PROFIT FIRST: POWERFUL TECHNIQUES TO BECOME A SUCCESSFUL ONLINE

USE THESE METHODS TO AVOID BANKRUPTCY ON YOUR WAY TO SUCCESS!

COLT FORTE

TABLE OF CONTENTS

INTRODUCTION

> "Successful people do what unsuccessful people are not willing to do. Don't wish it were easier; wish you were better" - Jim Rohn

Entrepreneurship. What does that word mean to you? Some of you reading this book might already have online business ventures, while some of you may struggle even to spell the word 'internet'. The rate at which things change in our world these days is accelerated, and the realm of online business is no different.

Making money on the internet has gone from being the domain of a few eBay resellers to now being dominated by multimillion-dollar companies. I'm not talking about the social media giants, either. I'm talking about a number of entrepreneurs who run successful e-commerce companies via websites they originally built for a fiver while lounging about in their gym shorts.

These days, the online world is saturated with wannabe entrepreneurs wanting to make some additional income. Let me make this crystal clear: This book is not for those who are looking for side hustle cash. It is for those who are serious about building their wealth and achieving financial freedom by putting in the work necessary to build a successful business.

Unfortunately, it still doesn't occur to some prospective entrepreneurs that an online business takes just as much work as a brick and mortar one does. This disease affects even those who own successful brick and mortar, physical businesses. Perhaps the low startup costs are a factor in this type of thinking. Needless to say, not taking the online arena seriously is akin to shooting yourself in the foot and then setting fire to it.

It'll take as much time and effort to start your business online as it will take to build a physical one. You will have days when nothing goes right. You'll have days when you do nothing and bank five figures in sales. The internet is not a magic bullet that will solve all your problems or make things easy. It is simply an opportunity that you need to learn how to grasp with both hands.

———

How to Use This Book

I have written this book with the intention of helping both first time, prospective entrepreneurs as well as veterans of the game who are not seeing the results they want or who wish to take their companies to the next level. The online world is an ever-changing beast, and it pays to stay up to date with everything that is going on out there.

This book will show you the ropes so you will be successful. Well, that sounds like a cliché, so let me explain further. Success in business, to me, is defined by the amount of profit you make. That's it. Everything in this book is designed to put more money into your pocket.

So how do you ensure more money flows into your pockets? Well, this is an interesting question. I could tell you exactly what steps I follow in my businesses and breakdown various sales channels and so on. But all of this is like me catching a fish and giving it to you. It'll feed you for a day at best.

A much better approach is to give you a framework and let you fill the colors in yourself. Everyone has different talents and make no mistake; you need to express your creativity to grow your business. What works really well for me might not work for you. Who knows, it might even be the worst thing for you to copy my methods exactly.

Thus, I will not be preaching to you about the exact, step

by step techniques in here. I will be giving you the principles you must follow to make money and the correct framework that must exist in order to execute your plans successfully. I will provide you with time tested and proven profit frameworks and methods to ensure your profit grows exponentially.

How you choose to execute them as part of your day to day plan is up to you. I assure you, none of the methods in this book are generic or obvious in any way. You will need to change your thought processes to make more money in your business, and I aim to open your mind to new methods in this book.

There is still a small issue, however. Why should you even listen to me?

————

Who is Colt Forte?

I'm sure you don't want me to waste your time with my biography here. A fact is that at one point in my life, I needed money. Like right now. I wasn't making much and believe it or not, my expenses were higher than my income, despite me cutting costs to the bone. I had heard that the internet was an easy place to make money and that all I had to do was to follow my passion, and it would come true. Well, I had nothing to lose, so I jumped right in.

Turns out that I had something to lose, and I did lose copious amounts of it. Money. The very last thing I could afford to lose. Thankfully, I had some money put away that allowed me to make my mistakes. Still, I was cutting it very close, scary close, actually with all my experiments with online businesses. I made good decisions, and I made poor ones. I bought courses from online marketing charlatans that were claiming to make a hundred thousand per month, and sometimes I signed up for their mentorships.

Eventually, one painful step at a time, I managed to start earning more and more from my online ventures. I managed to grow this business, and within a year, I had started my next one. Six months after that, my third venture took off, and I suddenly realized, I was one of those people making six figures in profit per month.

A mistake I made initially was in thinking that my problems would somehow disappear once I started making money. What happens is that you inherit new ones. Juicier ones. Ones you can sink your teeth into and improve yourself. You see, what changed my fortunes was the fact that I started chasing newer problems and figured out better solutions.

I am now a full-time online business consultant, aside from owning online business ventures, which earn me six figures a month in profit. My clients range from small entrepreneurs scrambling for cash, like how I once did, to multi-million dollar businesses looking to add to their bottom line. In fact, I guarantee my clients that I'll double their profits in the first year, I'm that confident of my methods.

Following your passion is essential, but that alone won't put food on the table. You need to learn how to turn a profit from it. Without a profit, your passion is going to turn into a source of pain. I guarantee it.

In this book, I'm going to give you all the tools you need to make a profit and then grow it. Follow the techniques and framework in here to the letter, even if it doesn't make sense to you at first, and watch as your business grows. You'll find that the chapters progress in complexity, and if you know you're familiar with a particular chapter's content, feel free to move on to the next one. I've written this book for everyone from beginners to veterans, but the latter might find some sections old news.

So, let's dive right in.

THE PROMISED LAND

Let's begin by first looking at what an online business really is and the nature of it. To many people, it seems daunting to start something on the internet. Since there's so much information out there, our brains get saturated really quick, and we only end up leaving with the impression that everything is too complicated.

Well, I'm here to tell you that starting an online business is the most profitable decision you will ever make in your life. The reason for this is simple: the promise of passivity.

ONLINE VS OFFLINE

In the olden days, meaning as little as two decades ago, if you wanted to start a business, you had two options. You could either do it part-time and run it using your phone, say a mail-order catalog business, or you could schlep over to the bank and convince the loan officer of how amazing your business plan was and why the demand for custom painted trash cans was genuine.

The physical business world hasn't changed much since those days. The startup costs are high, and you cannot run such a business part-time by holding down a secure job that pays your bills. This, of course, increases your financial risk since not only do you need to invest money into your venture, you also need to forego the income that it brings. Failure has a very high cost.

Of course, the part-time business option was always available before the internet, as well. However, you would have been limited in terms of customer reach. If you loved baking pies and had time on the weekends to prepare a batch, you could sell them in your neighborhood or to a few bakeries and stores nearby.

You could have brought in a few hundred dollars in sales per month, and that would have been that. The internet, however, has changed everything.

———

Reach

If you bake awesome pies, it is now possible to access not just your neighborhood but the entire world in only a few clicks. Suddenly, your potential customer base has increased from a few thousand to pretty much the whole population of the world, which is around seven billion, give or take a few million.

The best part of all this is the flexibility the internet gives you. You don't need to open a physical store or rent real estate to advertise your business. Online real estate, which I would argue is even more valuable than physical real estate these days when it comes to business, costs close to nothing. For as little as a few dollars per year, you can capture your own piece of the web and start a business!

The best part of all is this: You don't even need to be

awake to make money. Your website, which is just online real estate, will run while you sleep, and you can continue to sell and bank profits automatically. You don't need to wake up early and open your store, clean the premises, make sure display cases are attractive, and that your signboard works.

Online business places full control in your hands, and you get to set the clock. You can choose to work in the mornings or if you're a night owl, work all night! All the while, your store is open for business, and it runs itself. You don't need to worry about salespeople not doing their jobs and dealing with their problems.

Most importantly though, online businesses reduce your

financial risk significantly.

———

Risk

I've always thought of entrepreneurs as being risk assessors. A good entrepreneur or business person is one who handles uncertainty well. An unsuccessful business is a sign of its owner(s) not managing risk well. Risk management underlines everything in business. Now, I don't mean to say that you need to be pessimistic and worry about a meteor striking your home all the time.

What I mean is that every action you take should be evaluated from a risk-reward perspective. I'll talk about this later in chapter four, but for now, I'd like you to keep in mind the risk reduction capabilities of online businesses.

Starting a business on the internet requires very little money. Mind you; I'm saying money, not capital. Capital refers to the entire investment you will need to make to ensure success and is different from money needed for expenses and startup costs. So, make sure you don't confuse the two.

A website requires you to pay for a domain and hosting, along with a professional email address. You don't need to hire an expert designer for your store, thanks to easily customizable templates. You'll find some for free and others you need to pay for, but again, even the paid ones do not cost more than fifty dollars a pop. In fact, your template, should you choose to pay for it, is likely going to be your most significant upfront expense. Good luck opening a physical store by spending a maximum of fifty dollars!

You can start your business without having to sink huge costs upfront. Given the twenty-four-hour nature of your website, you don't need to be physically present while it runs. With just a functioning email address and an end of the day routine where you check your business emails for order notifications and implement them. Depending on your business model, you might not even need to produce anything and simply pass the orders along to your suppliers and have them fulfill everything.

This means, as your business grows, you can continue to hold your fulltime job and not give up that income. Thus, you're free to run your business with an open mind and will not be in the desperate position of having to make money from your fledgling business. Business income will vary according to seasonality, and as such, it is doubtful your business will make as much money in the first month as you do from your regular job.

This also brings me to a critical point about the nature of online businesses. You can make them as passive as possible. Do you know the number one key to getting rich? It's passive income. Income that keeps coming in while you sleep and income that takes care of itself, multiplying regularly and with little maintenance.

Real estate rental income is one way to earn passive income, but purchasing a piece of property is a significant investment. With the right online business, you can choose your preferred level of activity, whether you want to do it full time or whether you want to use it as a passive income source. This flexibility is something no physical business will ever give you. Not to mention, passive businesses make you far more money than the old passive income models.

———

Flexibility

Every business gives you the flexibility of being your own boss. With enough income pouring in, you can choose to work from where you want and when you want. However, the threshold of reaching this sort of lifestyle with a physical business is very high indeed. Think about it: you need to have multiple physical locations, each needs to be managed by employees, with more employees on top to manage the managers.

The number of people who manage to live such a lifestyle while owning physical businesses tend to be billionaires; that's how high the threshold is. The vast majority of physical business owners are tied down to their establishments and cannot afford to take a day off. Ask any restaurant owner, even successful ones, and they'll tell you how it really is. I don't mean to say such people are secretly fed up with their businesses, just that if you want location and time freedom, you cannot expect it from a traditional biz.

With an online business, this is different. Your threshold to achieve location and time freedom is determined by the lifestyle you want, not by what your business needs. For example, if you wish to travel the world, living in a location for a few months, and then moving on, you could choose to backpack or travel in luxury. Both options have different costs.

My point is, these costs are entirely up to you. Your business requires very little maintenance, and its costs will likely below. If your business is successful, your marketing costs will come directly from revenue automatically. Thus, you are in total control of your spending and can choose your lifestyle based on what you want. You don't need to be worth a lot of money to pay for your business needs and then pay yourself appropriately.

The flexibility an online business gives you manifests itself in other ways. For example, let's say when traveling or doing whatever it is you want to do, you spot a gap in the market and a problem that needs to be fixed. Given the potential customer-base you have, which is the whole world, you can easily pivot and tap into new markets without having to change too many things.

For example, if you decide to sell widgets in America primarily and find that your sales are not great, you could choose to sell them in India, where a growing economy is driving widget demand. What will this cost you? Close to nothing! And I don't mean ten thousand dollars' close to nothing', I really mean a few dollars at most. You simply need to fix a few parameters in your advertising and have that money come from sales! It is that simple.

———

Portability

The power of utilizing the internet for business has seeped into the traditional business world as well. More and more physical businesses are choosing to restrict their advertising to just online channels. The advent of pop up stores within the retail sector is a clear indicator that physical retail is on its last legs. Amazon dominates the retail space, and many large-scale companies have been relegated to mere suppliers for the online giant.

There are many businesses that have chosen to change tracks completely and become exclusively online ones. Even more drastically, a number of physical retailers are now prioritizing just their app and while they do possess online real estate such as a website, they see greater scope for the future with their apps (Gazdecki, 2018)!

Such flexibility is almost unprecedented in the business world, and while it may seem there are many businesses that have successfully mastered this, the truth is that everyone is learning as they go along. Our world is changing at a much faster pace, which means people need to cope with a faster flow of information to simply maintain the status quo. This is a good thing for you.

It means there are new possibilities and niches being born every second, and the days of one major company capturing and dominating a sector are close to over. The online business model ensures that competitiveness is constant, and even within saturated industries, the existence of sub-niches and sub-genres means a decent profit, thanks to the exposure and customer reach you will have.

Now, the only question that is left: What are you waiting for?

WHAT'S YOUR REASON?

Every first step involves the crucial act of dealing with fear. Many people seem to think that fear is something to be overcome, but it isn't. Fear never disappears completely. It's just your ability to live with it that increases. If you've always wanted to make more money and run a business, all of a sudden, your usual excuses have been rendered moot, and you now need to come face to face with the main reasons for you not taking action. I mean, if someone came by and gave you a chance to have full time and money freedom, wouldn't you take them up on it?

Instead, what people usually do is run through a laundry list of excuses and convince themselves they'll never be able to run an online business successfully. Well, let's take a look at some of the most common ones.

___

Money

"I simply don't have the money!" is a common refrain I hear from first-time clients all the time. Look, here's the deal. Online businesses vary in nature, much like traditional businesses do, except there are far more opportunities online. There are so many that I could fill an entire book with them by simply listing them out!

There are online businesses that require you to have substantial capital in order to ensure success. However, there are also businesses that do not require a single cent to begin. Here's the thing: technically, not a single online business requires you to invest more than what you pay for a cup of coffee at your local coffee shop.

Does this mean you should do it? Well, it depends on the business and the niche it is in. If you're looking to start an e-commerce store in the extremely competitive fashion clothing niche, you'd be daft to do so. But if your niche happens to be a relatively untapped and obscure one? Then you'll be fine.

You see, the economics of online business depends on the niche and the model, not just the type of business you're running. You can spend millions on an affiliate marketing business, or you can spend next to nothing. The choice is yours. So, you not having the money is a terrible excuse because guess what? You wouldn't hesitate to purchase a cup of coffee, would you?

No, the reason for your lack of action must be something other than the lack of money.

———

Knowledge

"I can't figure out this fancy internet stuff, I'm not a computer gal!" is another common refrain. Look, you need to be a technology geek to run an online business about as much as you need an engineering degree to drive a car. The reason you think this is a valid excuse is that you've probably read a few blogs and strategies and have been overwhelmed with a bunch of meaningless jargon.

Learning a new skill, like running an online business, is a step-by-step process. One of the shortcomings of Google is that it doesn't provide this step by step framework and instead throws everything at you all at once. It's a bit like attending your first class in college and the professor going through four year's worth of material in just an hour. There's no way you'll learn anything.

As a beginner, though, how would you determine a framework within which to learn? Well, this is where mentoring and courses come in. It is when a presumably successful online entrepreneur teaches you the wheel instead of you having to reinvent it. The problem is that this being the internet world we're talking about, there's no shortage of scumbag scam artists whose sole objective is to separate you from your money.

I take special pride in being able to identify such scam artists. It isn't because I'm more intelligent than the average person. It's because I have had extensive experience being ripped off by such people. Here's the thing: As a beginner, you do not need any individual mentoring. You need to simply read a book, much like this one, and learn the basics.

You will need special mentoring only when you want to make those additional, marginal gains to your business. I'm talking about adding a few percentage points more to your bottom line. In such cases, the people seeking help are already very successful, and those marginal gains translate to significant amounts for their incomes.

I advise any beginner who wishes to hire me as a consultant to simply go read a book first and to then take a stab at running a business. Only then do I accept them as clients since there's no point in you spending that money on me instead of gaining real-world experience. It's a bit like learning how to drive a car without actually doing it.

Once you've tried to do it and have run into an obstacle, an instructor can come in and teach you how to get past it. If you don't even have a concept of what a vehicle is, there's not much you stand to gain by hiring an instructor, is there?

You've taken the correct first step by purchasing this book, so you'll soon have all the knowledge you need. Despite this, some people still don't take action. Why is this? Don't say "I have a full-time job," because I've already shown you why that is a rubbish excuse.

What's the real reason? It's not money, and it's not knowledge for sure.

————

The True Reason

Here's the thing: Your current mental framework doesn't know how to handle an environment where anything is possible. A chaotic environment. The business world is a chaotic one, in the sense that your effort doesn't always equal your results. Sometimes you do everything right and still lose money.

This is in direct contrast to the way we're raised from childhood. Since we were kids, we've been conditioned to think that if we give the right answers on exams, we'll score more points. More points equal to higher grades, and better grades mean more plaudits. Those of you who played sports dealt with the same sort of thing there as well.

The more you worked on your game, your skills increased, and the better you played on the field. The better you play, the more trophies you won, and so on. These are examples of ordered environments where the reward and effort are equally aligned.

The business world is a chaotic environment where reward and effort are not aligned equally. You see, making money in business isn't about getting the answers right. It is about dealing with uncertainty. We're simply not taught to deal with this. Imagine an exam where the teacher tells you that even if you answer every question correctly, there's no guarantee you'll even pass the test, let alone score an A!

This is the sort of thing you sometimes will deal with in business. You can execute every step correctly and still lose money. The flip side is that it is equally possible to execute just one step correctly and make a ton of money. I mean, take Google, for example. How many failed projects have they had? Yet, would you think of them as failures?

Dealing with uncertainty is a function of your mindset, and I'm going to cover this in great detail in chapter three. For now, understand that your brain is playing tricks on you by creating a fear of the unknown. You already have everything to be successful and achieve your goals. You just don't know it yet.

You've taken the right first step. Now, it's time for you to acknowledge the real reason for your lack of action and to become aware of it. Don't reject it. You're scared, and that's OK. The solution to fear is knowledge, and that's what I'm going to give you throughout this book.

However, you need to come clean with yourself before proceeding further. A prosperous and free life awaits you. Don't let fear and ignorance hold you back!

MODELS - PART ONE

The first, and very important step you must take when deciding to start an online business is to decide what sort of a business you would like to get into. This involves educating yourself about the different business models out there. In this chapter, I'm going to break down the most lucrative online business models, along with some information about what to expect based on the amount of capital you have at your disposal.

Those of you who already run online businesses can safely skip this chapter. If you wish to gain some additional insight into how each model works, feel free to skip to that model's relevant section. If not, you can go ahead to chapter four, which deals with the mindset necessary for success.

For the rest of you, let's just dive in!

E-COMMERCE

E lectronic commerce or e-commerce simply refers to selling goods online. Which goods? Well, that's entirely up to you! The e-commerce model is extremely varied, so much so, in fact, that you could subdivide this into many of its own categories. These categories can be divided on the basis of which channel you wish to sell your products and also how you wish to source them.

So, let's first explore the basics of this model since every category of e-commerce shares these.

———

Niche

Every internet business eventually comes down to one thing: your niche. Niche selection is the first and most important step and goes a long way towards determining how well your business will do. Select the wrong niche, and no amount of hard work will bring you success.

So, what makes a good niche? Well, contrary to popular belief and practice, I don't have hard and fast guidelines for what a good niche is. I believe that your ideal niche is determined by your passion as well as your capital. Let me explain further.

Pursuing a niche that you're passionate about should make sense. I mean, it's going to take work to build a business so you might as well expend effort doing something you are interested in and are knowledgeable about. There is a further benefit to this approach since a lot of business, whether online or offline, is about solving problems.

The more interested and absorbed you are by a niche, the better your ability to discern problems and come up with solutions to it. Now, does this mean you should only pursue those niches you're extremely passionate about? Hardly. It all comes down to evaluating the demand within that niche for a particular problem or better service. I'll talk more about evaluation in a later chapter.

Maybe you are not familiar with what a niche is. Well, a niche is simply an interest. For example, sport is a niche, and sports, football, basketball, etc. are sub-niches. Depending on the size of the traffic an interest generates, you could tag a sub-niche as a niche. For example, college football and the NFL are both sub-niches within football, but both are popular enough to be niches in and of themselves.

Taking the college football niche, SEC football, Big Ten football, or PAC-12 football are sub-niches as are Notre Dame football, Alabama football, and so on. Generally speaking, don't get too caught up with niches versus sub-niches. I tend to designate smaller niches as sub-niches but this doesn't have any practical bearing on your business as long as you understand how the niches exist within the larger structure.

The important thing is that you understand the characteristics of your niche inside and out. Things such as average buyer personas, problems to be addressed, and possible solutions are some of the key points you should understand thoroughly. Now, if you're passionate about the niche, this should be straightforward, but you can complete this step via research, as well. I'll show you which key points you need to address in a later chapter.

For now, remember that niche selection is the bedrock upon which you'll build your e-commerce business, and it pays to spend a lot of time researching your niche. In fact, around 70-90% of your time should be spent researching your niche inside and out. Think of your niche as your location in a physical business. If there's no foot traffic, you're unlikely to succeed.

———

Product/Keywords

Once your niche is chosen, you need to select a particular product to sell. This product is going to have a name with which your prospective customers are going to search for on the internet. The search term that they use is called a keyword. Every product is going to have keywords associated with it.

For example, if someone wants to purchase a football jersey of the Alabama football team, they're probably going to search for "crimson tide football jersey" or "<playername> football jersey" or "Alabama football" and so on. By associating all of these keywords with your product, you'll ensure that it will be found easily when a person searches for your product.

Keywords that contain multiple words are called long-tail keywords. For example, "Alabama crimson tide foot- ball jersey 2019" is a very specific and descriptive keyword. A person searching for this keyword has a very defined intent, which is to say that they know exactly what they want.

A keyword such as "Alabama football" isn't very specific. We don't know whether this user wants a jersey or whether they're looking for tickets or some other information. Keep this in mind when you learn about the concept of the sales funnel in chapter five. For now, remember that long-tail keywords form the lifeblood of your business and are the most important things to define once you've picked a product.

———

Sourcing

Sourcing is the first point at which you will sub-categorize your e-commerce business. You can choose to sell either your own products, manufactured by you, or sell those produced in someone else's factory. The latter method is called dropshipping and is an extremely lucrative and popular business model.

With the former model, which is where you produce the goods yourself, you will have the advantage of having a unique product in the market. If you're artistic and love creating things, you'll love this approach. There are a number of business people who make lots of money operating this way. Your inventory and production costs will be higher, but your customers will likely be more loyal if your product is good. A good example of unique products you can see on the tv show Shark Tank. There you see how people developing unique products that they come up with and are very passionate about.

This is not to say that dropshipping customers won't be loyal. If your product is unique and differentiated enough in the market and if you pursue good marketing practices, you will have excellent demand from your customers.

Popular dropshipped items include pet accessories, clothes, watches, shoes, household items, and so on.

If you browse through Facebook a lot, you'll probably notice ads from websites that sell clothes and such products. These are dropshipping businesses where the products are manufactured at a factory and are shipped to you directly. In fact, let's take a detailed look at dropshipping.

───────

Dropshipping

Dropshipping has actually been around for ages now and first became popular with eBay. In this business model, a factory or manufacturer of goods allows you to market their goods, using your own brand name, and upon receipt of an order, will ship it directly to the customer. Thus, you only need to worry about marketing the product effectively and need not worry about storage and other shipping hassles.

You have zero inventory costs and make a profit based on the difference between your selling price and the manufacturer's cost. The manufacturer benefits from this because their expertise lies in making the product and not in marketing it. You're effectively their marketing arm, and you get to earn a percentage on the product's selling price.

Each manufacturer will have a number of such e-commerce dropshippers working for them, and thus they get a full-fledged marketing wing for no additional cost. From your perspective, what you need to do is focus on marketing and setting up good marketing channels, and you earn a commission. Everybody wins! There are a few drawbacks to dropshipping, though. First, you need to make sure the factory is reputable and will actually ship goods on time. A lot of dropshipping websites have this problem. In this age of Amazon next day shipping, typical dropshipping times take up to two and sometimes three weeks.

Very few customers will wait around for that long, so you need to factor that in when you choose your products. Will a customer wait around for a ballpoint pen for three weeks? Likely not. What about a customized chain for their dog? Very likely.

The other major issue you'll have to deal with is the inventory management abilities of the manufacturer and their ability to ship on time. This is where a second model of dropshipping enters.

Amazon FBA

FBA stands for fulfilled by Amazon. With this service, Amazon warehouses your product and ships it when orders are received for it from their website. FBA is an excellent option for a lot of dropshippers since it removes the need for a website. Instead, what you do is you list the product on Amazon's website and leverage the massive traffic that they receive.

Amazon is basically the Google of shopping. You can bet that every person searching for something on Amazon wants to buy it. This is an excellent situation from a sales funnel view, which I'll explain in detail later. For now, just keep in mind that buyer intent on Amazon's website is extremely high.

Contrast this with an average user on your own website. First off, you're not going to receive anywhere near the traffic that Amazon does. Secondly, your brand name is not going to be as strong as Amazon's, so the customer is less likely to trust your product. Lastly, you'll need to take care of customer service and billing, which involves employee costs. With FBA, you don't need to worry about all this.

FBA has its drawbacks, of course, with the biggest being Amazon's sometimes bipolar policies towards its suppliers. However, if you choose the right product, you will make a lot of money for very little expense.

———

Shopify

If you choose to build your own website, Shopify is your go-to destination. This platform is like a website builder but only for e-commerce. Thus, your payment gateways and supplier connections are all built-in via plugins. What's more, you can connect your Amazon store to Shopify and not have to maintain separate inventories.

Shopify also works directly with Oberlo, which is a prominent dropshipping software. Using this software, you can import your goods' listings as a batch from wholesale websites like AliExpress and list them on your website. Once an order is placed, Oberlo automatically pays the manufacturer and passes the order onto them.

It will also show you status updates as to the progress of the shipment and track any returns, along with remaining inventory for each item. All in all, Oberlo is an indispensable app for dropshipping purposes, although you only need this if you're running your own website. For strictly Amazon FBA, you only need to monitor your inventory with Amazon and place orders with your manufacturer before stock runs out.

This concludes our brief introduction to the e-commerce business model. In terms of capital required, if you have the right product, you can start for as little as twenty dollars per month. However, assuming good product selection, it is better to start off with around $5000 to leave some budget for testing product viability and advertising, since you shouldn't expect to pick winners right off the bat.

In terms of revenue, with good product selection, you can expect cash flows of around $3-4000 per month, so your return on investment is excellent. However, much depends on your product selection. You could also invest six figures into this model but even there, your product selection will be crucial. You can expect proportional revenues per month as with your investment.

KINDLE PUBLISHING

Amazon kindle publishing or KDP as it's called is an excellent starter business, and in fact, it is this online business that I recommend every newbie to get into first. This is because it is entirely platform-based, and the processes to follow are pretty straightforward. There isn't a lot of guesswork, or shall we say, 'artistry' required when it comes to figuring out how to advertise your products.

Your products, in this case, are books. You can sell e-books, paperbacks, and audiobooks. There are two selling platforms if you wish to sell exclusively on Amazon, but a number of others should you choose to be non-exclusive. In my personal experience, the other platforms are not worth the investment since Amazon pretty much dominates the space. You can pick up some residual income from those other sources, but don't make them your primary source of income.

Within KDP, there are two kinds of book publishing you can do: no/low content books and regular books. Let's look at them in order.

———

No or Low Content Books

These books, as their name suggests, don't have much within them. They range from ruled notebooks and journals to writing prompt books to fitness and diet tracking journals. Such books' demand depends on seasonality, with the holiday season and back to school seeing the highest number of sales.

There are virtually no limits on what sort of no content books you can publish. For example, you could publish a gratitude journal or a blank sketchbook for artists; the choice is yours. Like with every other e-commerce model, niche and keyword selection are absolutely crucial.

The good news with KDP is that instead of searching the entire web for good keywords, you can restrict yourself to just Amazon. For a good keyword selection you need to take a couple of important steps, and all of these are at the heart of choosing a good business model. I will delve into these topics in great detail in chapter four. For now, just remember the fact that you need to choose profitable keywords.

Amazon gives you this information for free via their BSR or bestseller rank. Every item on the website is assigned a number on the basis of how well it sells, depending on the category it is in. You can use the Kindle Spy Chrome Extension to see what a BSR number for a book is and how much revenue it makes per month.

Low and no content books do need some creative effort in that you need to make the covers yourself. You could outsource this to a freelancer, but it is unlikely you'll turn a profit if you do so. The reason is that publishing such books is a numbers game. You need to simply throw as many books against the wall and see what sticks.

The more books you have published, the better. Creating the covers is straightforward using software like Photoshop or even Canva and Gimp, which are free. The interiors can be created in MS Word, or Google slides and converted to a PDF format. From there, it is a simple upload on the KDP platform, and you're good to go.

Remember, the key to this is keywords and nothing else. Simply research good keywords using the business principles I'll show you in chapter five and apply them to the keywords you will search for on Amazon's website. Publishing no and low content books requires zero upfront investment and only needs time. To earn an income of one thousand dollars per month, you need to have published, conservatively, two hundred books. This sounds like a large number, but remember that these books are simply lined journals in most cases.

The interiors can be created within ten minutes, and your keyword research for a particular niche will take about a day. Once this is done simply release your books into the relevant keywords and repeat the process for every niche you can think of. Examples are gratitude journals, fitness journals, diet trackers, composition notebooks, teacher's notebooks, and planners, cardio and CrossFit journals, and so on.

———

Nonfiction and Fiction Books

Publishing nonfiction and fiction books take more investment but will make you more money over the long term. These are also subject to seasonality, but the income you will earn per month from these books, on a per book basis, is far more than no content books. I usually recommend people get started with nonfiction and then move into fiction books.

I would like to make clear that I'm talking about publishing books, not writing them. If you're a writer and if the idea of making money from publishing content offends you, then this book is probably not for you I'm afraid. I'm not going to talk about how you can become a better writer and build a fan-base; I'm talking about publishing for profit.

Now that the sentimental artists have left the chat let's move on. You will need to begin by researching niches and keywords again, like with no content books. Once you've researched these keywords, you will now need to write content for them. This is where the artists will get offended. I suggest using ghostwriting companies who will charge you around eight hundred dollars per thirty thousand words.

You will own the copyright to these books, and your next task is to promote them. It usually takes some time for the books to be written, and in that time, you need to build an email list of people who you think will be interested in your book. You could also reach out to book groups on Facebook and agree to leave a review for another author's book in exchange for leaving one on yours.

Thus, when you release your book, you will have some purchases lined up by prospective reviewers, and your book will rise in the BSR stakes. Amazon helps you promote your books by giving you five free promotion days, where your book can be priced for free, every ninety days. This can be done by choosing to enroll in KDP select when setting up your book.

This applies to eBooks and not paperbacks. However, Amazon links your paperback and eBook versions, so if your eBook rises in the rankings, you will see an increase in paperback sales as well.

The channel to sell your audiobooks on is called ACX. Currently, ACX is open only to residents of North America and the UK since presumably, Amazon thinks the rest of the world has the plague. Either way, there's no arguing with this policy, and you have to abide by it, whether you like it or not. On the ACX platform, you can find narrators who will produce your book and upload it on there. You will then need to review the narration, and once it passes the ACX QA process, your book will believe and will be linked to your eBook and paperback versions. You will also receive promo codes that allow people on your email list to receive the book for free, and you can request them to leave you reviews.

Capital Required and Downsides

Content publishing on Amazon generates more income, but it requires a higher amount of capital than low content book publishing. Much higher. While a single book costs around $1000 to produce (writing plus narration for a thirty thousand word book), it doesn't pay to release just one book at a time. This is because you'll find that most books will sell well for seven to eight months and then drop off.

Your best sellers will sell for around a year before dropping off in sales. In addition, some keywords will not be successful, and given the investment, the cost of mistakes is much higher. Thus, taking all of this into account, I would say do not venture into this field with anything less than $15,000 as capital. This will provide for around fifteen books and will ensure that the income you receive from the books can be reinvested to produce more books.

You can expect a good book to provide you with $250 per month in income in total. A decent book should bring in around $100, and anything less than that is a failed release. Also, it is essential that you reinvest all your revenue back into the business until you cross the $10,000 per month mark, at which point you should not withdraw more than 20% of revenue to pay yourself.

This is because the greater the number of books you have, the faster you can grow your business, and the more money you'll make. KDP is a great way to make $20-30,000 per month, but you will need to master keyword research and reinvest constantly. Once you're above

$15,000 per month, you can withdraw half that amount and pay yourself.

The biggest downside to this business is that you are completely at Amazon's mercy and make no mistake; Amazon is a draconian landlord. The slightest transgression or even a hint of you breaking their terms of service will result in an account ban that cannot be contested.

ACX is particularly strict in this regard, with publisher and author support being virtually non-existent.

I mean, there is a number you can call, but they usually are of no help and will not assist you when it comes to more complicated queries about your account status or the status of a book. So, you need to make sure you follow the rules at all times.

If you can do that, then KDP is a wonderful income stream. Just make sure you're well-capitalized and don't attempt it with less capital than what I recommended. This is from my own experience and mistakes that I made when I started out with KDP. Don't repeat them.

Let's now look at some more online business models.

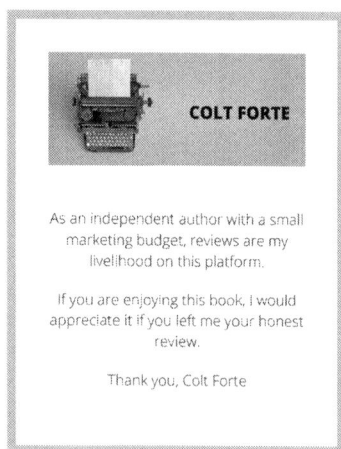

COLT FORTE

As an independent author with a small marketing budget, reviews are my livelihood on this platform.

If you are enjoying this book, I would appreciate it if you left me your honest review.

Thank you, Colt Forte

MODELS - PART TWO

We've looked at E-commerce and KDP as two very profitable online business models thus far. There are three more business models that are extremely profitable, and if done right, can make you seven figures per year.

So, let's look at them now.

AFFILIATE MARKETING

Affiliate marketing is probably one of the more common ways people make money online. While e-commerce and KDP necessarily require you to have a hardcore business mindset to succeed, affiliate marketing can be done on the side for some additional cash quite successfully.

What I mean to say is that if you wish to make some side income and are not looking for financial and time independence particularly, then affiliate marketing will provide you with the best bang for your buck. The previous two business models require you to keep scaling and building it, or else, you'll find your income stalling and keeling over.

Now, there might be some of you who are wondering what affiliate marketing even is? Well, let's define it first.

———

What it is

Let's say you walk into a clothing store and see that they've got some pretty good stuff. It just so happens that you know a bunch of people who are looking for exactly this type of thing, and you know they're going to purchase it, given the chance. So, being the enterprising individual that you are, you walk up to the owner of the store and tell them that you'll be able to shift their inventory for them in return for a commission on the sales.

Here's the thing: Most physical businesses will never accept such an offer for a variety of reasons. However, this sort of transaction is quite common in the online business world. This is what affiliate marketing is all about. You are effectively the marketing and sales executive for a particular online product or service and on every sale that you refer to the merchant, you earn a commission.

The great thing about affiliate marketing is that it is action-based. What this means is that while the majority of affiliate programs pay you on the basis of sales generated, there are a number of programs that pay you on the basis of leads generated. Each program will have a different method of defining what a 'lead' is. Some may say a lead is a person who fills out a contact form, and another might say a lead is someone who schedules an appointment.

Either way, most affiliate marketing programs are referred to as CPA or cost per action programs. The action can be a purchase or anything else, such as filling out a form. The amount of commission paid depends on the merchant. For example, Amazon has the biggest affiliate marketing program on the plant, thanks to the number of products they sell and payout on average, 7% per sale.

There are merchants who payout 50% commissions as well, but their product prices will be low. Then there are products which sell for thousands of dollars which payout 5% and are extremely lucrative. It is best to focus on the amount of commission you will make per action, instead of the percentage when evaluating the profit potential of a program.

Another type of affiliate program is CPC/PPC or cost per click/pay per click. This is when you place ads on your website or content, and you earn money when someone clicks the ad. Now, this is not a book dedicated to affiliate marketing, so I don't have enough space to delve into the specifics of this. Long story short, stick to CPA offers.

CPC usually requires a ton of traffic to earn good money because of the low payouts. If you're bringing in a ton of traffic, you might as well implement CPA since you'll earn exponentially more. This doesn't always hold up, mind you, but for the majority of cases, this is true.

Let's move on and look at how you can implement an affiliate marketing model.

————

Steps to Profit

Affiliate marketing first requires you to have an online channel or medium. This could be a blog, a YouTube channel, an Instagram account, a Pinterest account, a Facebook account, anything on social media really that allows you to place an affiliate link and refer people to merchants. If you have an email list, you can market to this list by placing your affiliate link within the email.

An affiliate link is a unique link that you will receive when you set up an account with the merchant. You can sign up to an affiliate marketplace where you'll be able to pick from a number of merchants, or you can check merchants individually. You will then place this link throughout your preferred medium, and when anyone clicks the link and performs the action necessary, you earn a commission.

Affiliate programs usually require certain hoops for you to jump through, such as a minimum amount of traffic and so on. Some will require you to have a website; some will require that you promote only through certain channels and so on. Read the conditions carefully and evaluate whether you'd like to work with the merchant or not.

Now that we've covered the basics let's look at which channels you should use the most.

————

The Best Channels

I'll keep this short. Use Instagram and YouTube. Pinterest is a great channel as well, but I personally find it a bit clunky to use. IG and Pinterest are excellent options for affiliate marketing since they're both visual mediums, and people connect with images better than a wall of text. The days of starting a blog and monetizing it easily are long gone. People don't like reading anymore, as evidenced by the boom in audiobooks.

YouTube plays into this as well since it's a visual medium. However, with YouTube, you will need to create video content which takes time, and YT is generally more competitive. Please understand I'm not talking about monetizing your channel through YouTube, which is another type of income stream. I'm talking about referring your subscribers to affiliate links.

YouTube plays very well into influencer marketing, but this takes time to build up to. Pinterest and IG are far easier to break into, and you will find higher engagement rates for far lower profile credibility. What I mean is that people will only buy from people they find credible. Given the nature of IG and Pinterest, it's a lot easier to establish this credibility since the threshold is lower. On YouTube, it takes a bit longer.

———

Investment and Income

If you wish to implement affiliate marketing as a business successfully, you will need to invest around $2000 upfront in advertising and other costs. With such an investment, and assuming you do everything else correctly, you can expect to earn up to $4-5000 per month within three to five months.

Admittedly, there is a lot contained within the 'do everything else correctly' portion involving your own credibility, the time you dedicate, your user engagement, and so on. However, once your initial efforts sees fruit, your user base only grows, and you'll see your income constantly increase.

Making five figures and even six figures per month requires you to sell high ticket or highly-priced products, and you need to be an influencer to do this. I'll cover this separately.

Remember that every platform has its own quirks, and you should take the time to study them carefully and figure out how to boost your income. It will seem intimidating at first, but trust me, it really isn't. If you're looking for some side income, remember that all the accounts on the channels mentioned are free, and you'll only need to spend time boosting them.

Thus, any money you make on them will provide a good profit margin. You just need to see whether the amount is worth the effort you put in.

INFLUENCER MARKETING

Becoming an influencer is much more difficult these days, but the payouts are terrific for the amount of time and money you need to invest. Influencers can be affiliate marketers or can sell their own products. The greater your credibility, the higher you can price your products.

The biggest factor in all of this is the level of trust you manage to build amongst your followers. Also, remember that a huge follower count is not a guarantee of big money. For example, a lot of travel influencers on IG find themselves without money at the end of the month, and usually, on that platform, it is only the older influencers who manage to make a sizable income of six figures per year.

.   .   .

In contrast, YouTube travel influencers tend to make a lot more than their IG counterparts since it is easier to document your own personality and style on video than on a single photo. In other words, it is somewhat easier to build trust on YouTube than the picture platforms.

Facebook is another excellent platform for building credibility thanks to its ability to create groups and interact with your users directly, which is a bit of a hurdle on IG and to a lesser degree, on YouTube.

The most famous influencers are, of course, the Kardashians and Jenners, with Kylie Jenner becoming a billionaire thanks to her large IG follower count and marketing her makeup brand to them. You will often find a lot of supermodels and such doing the same thing by setting up their own skincare or cosmetics brands and marketing them to their followers.

This brings me to a good point.

————

Platform of Choice

I touched on this in the previous section on affiliate marketing. Remember that each platform has its quirks and its own typical user behavior. People on IG behave differently than they do on Facebook, even if it is the same person. Thus, when choosing your platform, which is of extreme importance if you wish to go down the influencer route, you need to take this into account.

For example, if you're a guy and wish to become a fitness influencer and decide to use IG, you might as well give up right now. However, if you're an attractive woman, go for it. This doesn't sound politically correct but it is a fact and is backed up by data (Fowler, 2017). As a guy, if you wish to become a fitness influencer, you're better off on Facebook and YouTube.

Similarly, if you're a guy trying to break into the men's fashion game, IG is extremely important for you, as is YouTube. However, if you keep your videos long-winded and don't get to the point quickly, you'll find a lot of guys tuning out. Generally, on YouTube, advertisements are annoying so perhaps, it's not a good thing to monetize your channel. A number of extremely successful business influencers, like Grant Cardone and Dan Lok do not monetize their YouTube channels since they sell high ticket products by providing great content.

———

Monetization

By becoming a credible influencer, you can easily rake in six figures a month by affiliate marketing, such as selling courses, or by selling your own products. A rising trend has been to create mastermind groups for other influencers, those less successful than you, and to charge five figures each for the chance to network.

Every businessperson knows the importance of networking and will jump at the chance. However, it all starts with credibility. Now, you could either be genuine when it comes to establishing this, or you could fake it till you make it.

The latter approach is adopted by a number of influencers, and some key things to look out for are the presence of luxury sports cars (usually rented) and pretty girls (also hired). As an aside, it has become quite lucrative to become a model who appears in such influencers' videos with a number of young women earning five figures a month via this approach.

Which approach you choose to take is up to you. Obviously, I recommend being genuine since, aside from being the right thing to do, it's just good business in the long run. Pick a niche you love and then run with it. Yes, I'm recommending you follow your passion here since influencing requires a lot of credibility, and passion is the best way to generate this.

How much will you need to invest? Well, this is impossible to put a number to but suffice to say that it will cost you a bit. Thus, make sure you have steady income streams in order to invest repeatedly back into this. Over the long run, you will be able to establish credibility and earn big bucks.

Whatever you do, do not expect to make large amounts of money with little to no investment. The world just doesn't work like that.

I'm thinking to do something with seniors → Laundry - shopping - driving to appointments etc.

SERVICE BUSINESSES

E veryone everywhere wants something. So why not give it to them? All right, this is about as vague as you can get when it comes to a business idea, but my point is that there are such a large number of things that people need, you could go on forever coming up with specific ideas.

Here are a number of examples I can think off the top of my head. Pet grooming services, pet care services, services in your area of expertise, business setup services, laundry pickup and drop off services, grocery delivery services, offshore bank account and company services, retirement and residency services, and on and on.

If you're noticing a pattern in those examples, I provided they have a few things in common. One, all of them can be run through a middleman. In other words, you don't need to actually do any of the legwork and can outsource them to employees or other agencies. Second, all of them can be done via a website or an app. Third, all of them pay fat margins or are emotionally important to people.

your thoughts

In a nutshell, this is the key to establishing an online service business. You need to address something that is emotional for your customers and something that has good margins. In addition, a good business will adhere to your lifestyle so you can either do it yourself or outsource it.

To be honest, service businesses tend to follow trends, but there are some evergreen ones out there. Anything involving pets is an evergreen niche. The downside is that such niches tend to be oversaturated, and it can be difficult to beat your competitors. The net result is that your initial investment will need to be higher if you're taking on an established competitor.

A key feature of online businesses is their geographical reach. With services, this can be tricky to achieve since a lot of them will be delivered to your local area. If you have an existing physical business that provides a service, simply migrating everything online is a good option. For those looking to get started, though, don't pick something that restricts your options unless the demand is exorbitant.

———

Lucrative Models

The best service-based businesses for those starting out are those which can be outsourced and ones that you earn a good margin from. For example, not many outside the field are aware of this, but providing offshore company setup services is an extremely lucrative niche.

The key within this niche is credibility, and this can be established via an informative website. You can outsource the actual work to lawyers and agents who take care of the paperwork, and you can earn either a commission from them, or you can charge your clients a fee upfront. If you are even slightly knowledgeable about this field, there's a lot of money to be made.

Another good option is to freelance with your skills. If you're a writer or an SEO specialist, you can advertise your services on freelance websites or market yourself on LinkedIn. Personally, I'd avoid freelance websites like Upwork or Fiverr like the plague since you'll only end up in a bidding war where the one who wins is the one who loses the most.

Instead, focus on networking via LinkedIn and other websites like Problogger (for writers) or Angieslist (for all skills) where your services will receive a higher level of respect and money. SEO is an especially lucrative skill to possess since everyone needs to be on the web these days. If you don't have this skill, consider investing in a course and classes to learn this because of its massive demand. Service-based businesses tend to lack the passivity that a lot of other online business models have, and I'd recommend looking into them only if it suits your personality and if your skills match up. If not, I'd stick to the other business types.

This brings to a close our look at profitable online business models. Remember that a lot of these models go way deeper than what I've listed on here. For example, with affiliate marketing, which is probably the deepest of them all, there are a number of ways to make money, and these methods can be subdivided on the basis of platform, launch timing, audience, and so on.

For example, did you know you can get paid while playing video games? It's true! You simply record your video game playing time, post it on Twitch, and if it's engaging enough, you'll earn money. You can then sell game skins or accessories via your channel and earn affiliate income. The number of pimpled teenagers doing this is evidence that it works. If you're still not convinced, there's even an eighty-three-year-old woman doing this. Head over to YouTube and search for 'Skyrim grandma.'

There is no end to online business ideas, and the most important thing for you to do is to explore which idea fits you the best. If something clashes with your personality, simply don't do it. There are so many business models out there; you're bound to find one that suits you. For example, if you're uncomfortable making videos with your voice and face on them, then don't try to be a YT influencer.

Match your personality with your preferred idea and platform!

YOUR MOST IMPORTANT TOOL

Wanting to become a successful entrepreneur is one thing. Actually, achieving it is a whole different ball game. As I mentioned earlier, you need to possess the right mindset to succeed. Your mindset is what determines your thoughts, and your thoughts feed into your actions. Needless to say, your action ultimately determines your level of success and failure.

Thus, mindset and beliefs are at the bottom of everything. One wrong or unsupportive belief can wreck things far more than an unfavorable economy or any external factor. What is a mindset though? Simply put, your mindset is the sum of all your beliefs, which have been ingrained over the years, thanks to your experiences.

. . .

Your beliefs are wired into your brain, thanks to your actions over the years. Stands to reason then that your actions and behavior moving forward will determine what sort of mindset you develop, doesn't it? In this chapter, I'm going to give you all the beliefs and actions you need to take in order to be successful.

You might struggle to implement this at the start, but with practice and over time, you'll be amazed at the difference these actions will make to your results.

WORK HARD

Yup, kind of obvious. We might get this one out of the way as soon as possible. Look, there is not an easy way to say this, but you're going to have to work. Work until you're dead tired, and all you need is a little dollop of sleep. And then you need to work some more.

Don't let anyone tell you not to; it is hard to get a business up and running. You're going to be on your own, despite the best wishes and support of friends and family since you're the only one who can take action. Your business is an extension of you, and only you can determine its level of success and failure.

Does this mean you need to keep working yourself to the bone constantly? No, not quite. The thing to do is to work smart and intelligently. There is a tendency amongst entrepreneurs to become workaholics. It stands to reason, after all. Entrepreneurs tend to be high achievers and are wired differently from the rest of the population (Long and Lieberman, 2018). What I mean to say is that they follow different habits, not that they're somehow born special. This often manifests as a need to do everything right and right now.

The desire to work must be balanced with the knowledge of being kind to oneself. Be kind to yourself and don't ignore your health, both physical and mental. Coupled with the correct approach to risk, you'll hit success, and your work will not feel like work.

LEAVE YOUR COMFORT ZONE

Your biggest enemy is not the economy or your mortal enemy if you're lucky enough to have one. It is the comfort zone. You see, your brain loves comfort. It doesn't have to learn anything new and can simply run things on autopilot. But your brain is also a good liar.

The reality is that it actually loves new challenges and learning new things. Its job is to simplify your life, and this is why it seeks to automate as many things as possible. Take in too much new stuff all at once, and it's going to scream in protest. Don't give it enough new stuff in proper time, and it grows stale.

The key to unlocking your brain's power is to keep

feeding it new challenges, bit by bit. This way, it gets its exercise in and stays fresh. You get to benefit from exposure to new challenges, and your ability to deal with new situations increases exponentially.

HARNESS THE POWER OF PASSION

I've said before that passion tends to be misinterpreted quite a bit by a lot of first-time entre-preneurs. 'Follow your passion and success is guaranteed!' scream the expert motivational speakers. Well, they all tend to leave out some important facts when talking about the topic.

First off, if you're passionate about your area of business and solution you're proposing, then go for it. This is great. However, if you look around and study the most successful business people, you'll notice that they don't necessarily tend to be the most passionate about their business' subject areas.

. . .

Take the example of Warren Buffett and Bill Gates. There's no doubt they're extremely passionate about the art of making money and technology, respectively. Then there's Sam Walton, the founder of Walmart. Was he passionate about groceries? Was Ray Kroc passionate about hamburgers?

I'm trying to highlight the mistake that a lot of first-timers make. They seem to think that unless you're passionate about your product or line of business, you should not even begin to attempt launching a business. This is simply not the case. The key is to be passionate about something.

Why are you starting a business? Is it to provide your family with a better quality of life? Is it to make more money and escape the rat race? Making money has become a curse word of late thanks to the business environment governments and big companies have foisted upon us. However, money does buy you freedom from time, location, and every day worries. There are hardly any more noble pursuits than you trying to give yourself a good life.

This is a great thing to be passionate about. Ask yourself what it is you wish to achieve with the money you will make from your business. At every waking moment, give this your attention, and you'll find yourself jumping out of bed every day, rushing to get to work.

LEARN ALL ABOUT RISK

I've mentioned before that entrepreneurs tend to be experts on judging risks. The difference between an entrepreneur's view of risk and a regular person's is that the former tends to weigh the reward as well, along with the risk. If the reward is worth the risk, go for it.

You see, business is a chaotic environment. It isn't some academic exam where if you get 90% of the answers correct, you end up with a 90% score. In business, 90% could result in no money made or some money made or a lot of money made. There are no guarantees.

Our brains are not naturally wired to deal with chaotic environments, so you need to understand that the only way to prosper in a chaotic environment is by setting the odds in your favor. Think of it as a game of blackjack, but with the odds in your favor. Yeah sure, you'll take a bad beat once in a while when the dealer happens to have a higher hand, but if the odds are in your favor, say 60/40, you'll win in the long run.

All you need to do is to keep doing the same thing that makes sure those odds remain in your favor. Thus, over time, despite those single hand losses, you'll come out ahead. Reread this section again, because understanding this will change your worldview on a lot of things.

Remember, it's all about the odds, not the certainty, of a result.

ESTABLISH TRUST

With yourself, that is. The person who matters the most to your business is you yourself. I don't mean to say this in a big-headed or egotistical way. It's just that you are the boss now and if you have employees, they will take their cues from you. How do you conduct yourself? How much do you back yourself in tough times? Do you throw in the towel easily or keep persevering?

You have been blessed with creative and analytical faculties that no other species on this planet has. We don't fully understand how the creative mechanism in our brain works yet. When our brains are relaxed, and our conscious mind is turned off, we tend to have flashes of inspiration and intuition. We create things out of thin air.

· · ·

Every human being is blessed with this, and it is imperative that you trust this. You have the tools necessary to ensure the success of your business, no matter how tough the situation is. Is there any scientific proof for all this? Well, actually there is!

In his groundbreaking book, *Psycho Cybernetics,* Dr. Maxwell Maltz proved that every living creature is genetically engineered for success (Maltz, 1960). For example, a young bird, once it's learned to fly, does not need to be told which way to fly for winter or which way warmth is. It simply knows and does it. Neither does it need to be told what sort of food is good for it, it simply eats. The same applies when it comes to nest building.

Where is this information coming from? Sure, some of it is from the environment, but even orphaned chicks tend to behave the same way. So, it is obvious that there is some part of every living being's brain that is encoded with some sort of information to help it succeed.

In the case of an animal, this is simply survival, but human beings are different. We have far more complex brains, and success to us means a lot more than survival. Thus, if less aware life forms have been given the tools to succeed, it stands to reason that human beings have as well.

Trust this information and use it to your advantage! Trust yourself; you got this!

TAKE MASSIVE ACTION

Sure, everyone tells you to take action, but I'm here to tell you to take massive action. A simple action isn't going to cut it. So, what is massive action? Well, think of everything that you need to be doing and amplify it by a factor of ten or a hundred. That's what you need to do to succeed.

This doesn't mean to say that success is something extremely tough and beyond your grasp, far from it. The beauty of massive action is that it brings you closer to your goal in record time as opposed to simply taking action. By getting there faster, you actually preserve vital energy and get injected with optimism. Not to mention, by getting to your goal faster, you can scale higher highs since you have more time on your hands.

Massive action is not an absolute thing. It is relative to

everybody. To a couch potato simply getting up, going to the gym and working out for an hour is massive. To someone who does it regularly, that's routine. You need to work out what your 'massive' level is and work accordingly.

Some days, you just won't feel up to it, and this is fine. Remember, you need to prioritize your own health, mental and physical. So, listen to and trust your body always. On such days, do whatever you can to keep taking steps forward.

———

Go Ahead and Fail

No, that's not a typo. I'm actually telling you to go ahead and fail. A poor relationship with failure is what keeps a lot of achievements from seeing the light of day. It's time for you to fix this relationship and recognize it for what it is.

We've already seen how every human being has the tools to succeed wired within them. One of the ways this ability to succeed comes to light is by making mistakes, which is just negative feedback. In his book, *Psycho Cybernetics,* Dr. Maltz uses the example of a self-guided torpedo as it makes its way towards its target.

As the torpedo gets launched, it receives negative feedback if it goes off course. The moment it receives this feedback, it corrects course and makes its way forward. The more off-target it gets, the more negative feedback it receives as it learns its way forward to its target.

Your progress towards your goal plays out the same way. Mistakes simply tell you how not to do something and failure is simply one way of not doing things correctly. So, embrace the fact that you failed and realize what it is teaching you.

———

Get Focused

Eliminate things from your life that don't add to your goal. Remove the sources of negativity and things that hold you back. Some of these will be painful, but remember why you're doing this in the first place. You need to do everything necessary to succeed, so don't underestimate the power of focusing on your goal.

If your reason to achieve your goal is emotionally positive enough, the focus will take care of itself. The things for you to do is to eliminate distractions and noise. Make it as easy for yourself to focus, and you'll find yourself working better and taking larger steps towards your goals as the days progress.

————

Set the Right Goals

I'm going to address goal setting in a later chapter, so don't worry, you'll get plenty of details there. As of now, just remember that your goals are what get you laser-focused in a single direction. Make sure your goals are big enough and bold enough to inspire you truly.

I've always maintained that if your goals don't cause you discomfort and if you don't ask yourself how on Earth you're going to achieve them, then your goals are wrong. If you know how to achieve them, then they aren't goals, they're just tasks. So, dream big.

————

Master Networking

Entrepreneurs like to think of themselves as lone wolves and tend to subscribe to the philosophy "if you want something to be done right, you have to do it yourself." Well, this is precisely the wrong way to do things. Even if you don't like it, you need the help of people around you.

Did you know that successful people, be it in an organization or in business, tend to have very high emotional quotients (Mindtools.com, 2019)? They have the ability to empathize and simply get along well with other people. This makes sense since it is other people who will open doors for you and introduce you to opportunities?

Establishing a good team and a network of likeminded people around you is essential. Our environment plays an important role in who we are as people, and if we surround ourselves with people who think small and don't take action, we'll turn into them. This is why the power of masterminding is so important, and every successful person knows this instinctively.

Surround yourself with successful people who motivate and inspire you and who you look up to, and you'll find yourself improving your lot in life.

———

Be Patient

Every "overnight" success story is in all reality, years in the making. It is the result of persistent and continuous effort and work. It involves discipline and repeated correction of mistakes. Trying to become successful with a get rich quick mindset is simply not going to work for you, so you might as well drop it now for your own sake.

The road can seem long and without an end, though. This will cause some feelings of despondency and nega-tivity. The thing to do is to break it down into chunks and to use your arrival at these chunks as a marker of sorts.

Even better is to break down your goals into the purpose, vision, and goal matrix.

This method is often proposed by the motivational speaker, Bob Proctor. Your purpose is what ultimately drives you and is your reason for existence. It is what motivates you to wake up in the morning and energizes you. Your purpose can change depending on where you are in your life, and this is fine. This is the high-level picture, so to speak.

Your vision is your roadmap to get to your purpose. It is the method you will use to reach and achieve your purpose, and this will also change depending on the level of negative feedback you receive. You will perhaps try to seek alternative routes along the way, and this is perfectly fine.

Your goals are what determine your progress along with your vision, and are the mile markers which inform you of how far you've come and where you're going. Achieving your goals in this manner will energize you and also enable you to focus on your journey and achieve the thing that's right in front of you, instead of worrying about the big picture and wondering how on Earth you're going to do everything else.

As an example, let's say you decide that you want to start an online business. Well, what is your purpose? Perhaps, the business is your way of ensuring you achieve full freedom in your life? Thus, your purpose is to live a life of freedom, both in terms of location and financially.

Next, your vision, which is how you'll achieve that purpose, is to start an online business that earns X amount of dollars per month. This is too vague, and you need to refine it a bit. So, let's say that your vision is to start a KDP business that earns X dollars per month so as to give you time and money freedom. You might expand into other businesses, but all of that can come later. For now, this is your vision.

What are your goals? Well, your first step is to make

$1000 per month. Then $3000, $5000, and so on until you reach your desired amount per month. Write down the actions you will need to take to reach the first goal and get to work by taking massive action!

This is a different approach to goal setting from the one I'll be giving you in a later chapter but is as effective. Use this to measure your progress and, more importantly, measure how far you've come along your path.

Remember that your mindset determines your level of success, so do not underestimate this component. A lot of people think that all they need to do is to do the right thing, and success arrives. Your actions are determined by your thoughts, so even doing the right thing requires you to think correctly.

Use the points in this chapter to set yourself up for

mental success. Your next step will be to evaluate business conditions using a simple step by step process. You can use this template to evaluate any business that is out there, whether online or offline since it adheres to principles that are common to every enterprise.

So, let's take a look at the profit path next!

THE PROFIT PATH

Business relies on a few fundamental principles for success. This pattern is repeated in each and every business you will see, whether it be physical or online, or if it is a logistics business or a flower delivery business. Remember how you learned that business is a chaotic environment? And that to succeed in a chaotic environment, you need to understand the patterns that occur and their odds?

Well, this chapter is about that pattern. Following these principles will not guarantee you success every single step of the way in your business. However, remember that you don't need success at every single juncture. What you need instead is to come out ahead in the overall picture. This is what probabilistic thinking is all about.

If this isn't making sense to you, please go back and read the 'learn about risk' section in the previous chapter. If it is making sense to you, let's move ahead!

THE PATTERN OF PROFIT

E xecuting these fundamental steps will ensure that not only will your business start well but will also ensure that over time, your profit will keep increasing, depending on the business' economics. Over time, the economics of a particular line of business will assert itself. For example, it is hard to imagine a flower delivery business making more money than an oil refinery.

However, this doesn't mean you cannot make money in the flower delivery business. In the long run, make sure you adjust your expectations to the overall economic picture of that line of business. When starting out and building it, though, these principles will make sure you get to that optimal, maximum profit point faster.

. . .

I've listed the things you need to take care of in a step by step pattern:

1. Evaluate the landscape
2. Define your niche
3. Build your sales funnel
4. Drive traffic
5. Provide value
6. Be visible
7. Drive repeat purchases
8. Learn the art of the upsell

Let's take a look at them one by one.

————

Evaluate the Landscape

Every great product ultimately has one thing in common: It provides an elegant solution. You see, if you're starved of ideas for a product or for a new service, you need to address your ability to look at problems. Problems come in all shapes and sizes but generally fit into one of three categories:

1. Problems without solutions thus far- These are the huge problems which have had no solutions offered up to solve them as yet. Examples include climate change, world peace, and so on. The problems don't have to be this broad. It could also be something like making LCD screens inherently more friendly to the eye.

2. Problems with imperfect solutions- These problems have solutions, but they're clearly stop gap ones. Examples include smartphone covers which only cover up the fact that smartphones are inherently fragile, unlike cell phones in the previous decade.

3. Problems whose solutions can be improved- This is where a solution already exists, but there is space for marginal improvement. Examples include updates to software or extensions.

Here's the thing: The profit potential of all of these problems are exactly the same. People tend to think that being a pioneer pays, but research shows that this is not the case (Grant, 2015). Unless you're incredibly passionate about the problem, don't attempt to be a pioneer. Companies like Microsoft, Apple, Google, Facebook, and Amazon are not pioneers, despite the impression they create these days.

.   .   .

Every problem which requires a solution will have other people attempting to solve it, along with you. You need to evaluate the competition to see whether you stand a chance against them. For example, if you have a revolutionary new way to conduct an online search, sorry to say, you're not going to stand much of a chance competing against Google.

However, if your competition is on the same level as you or slightly ahead, you can easily compete. Take the example of a KDP business. If you're just starting out as a publisher, do you think it's easier to compete in a keyword which has 10,000 results or 2,000? 2,000 or 100?

Another aspect of the competition is the number of players involved. If there are too many of them, the odds of your solution being first to market is lesser. Thus, choose to solve a problem where the number of competitors is low.

Lastly, correlate the competition to the demand. Sure, there might be a number of people trying to devise a solution, but is there a need for the solution in the first place? Entrepreneurs tend to get caught up with the need for a solution and forget to evaluate demand.

.   .   .

The best scenario for business success is devising a solution for which there is a great demand and where the competition is low (meaning they're on your level and are less in number). What is your level? Well, you need to be honest about your skills and evaluate yourself accordingly.

Sticking with the KDP example, if you're a publisher making $10,000 per month, it's safe to say you have the skills to dominate keywords with 10,000 results thanks to your body of work. If you're someone who makes $2,000 per month, not so much. Profit is your ultimate evaluation in business. If you're not making money, you're not skilled at it and should adjust your sights accordingly.

Lastly, look at the business economics. Sometimes, no matter what the situation is, you will struggle to make money in a particular line. A great example is the airline business. Yes, there's a huge demand for it. Yes, you could slot in as a regional airline and partner with the bigger ones. However, if you manage a net profit margin of 2%, you're doing a great job. All this is assuming you have the money to set one up in the first place.

.   .   .

There's a reason the best airlines in the world are all nationalized, and the most profitable ones are cut-rate flying buses. The economics are just rubbish, and you're better off diverting your energies elsewhere to generate a better bang for your buck.

———

Define Your Niche

Niche selection is something that goes hand in hand with the first step. As you evaluate problems, you will accordingly be looking at various niches. Deciding whether a niche is a good choice is pretty much the same as the previous step. You need to match the demand with the competition and see how your skills match up. I've already talked about this, so I won't go into detail.

The thing I would like to highlight here is that you ought to narrow down a niche to your competitive level. For example, if you're starting out, your niche should be as specific as possible, and as you grow in size, you can become more generic. Think of how Amazon grew its business.

It started off focusing on just books and nothing else. Then came AWS, retail, then Prime, Prime TV, the Fire

Stick, Alexa, Groceries, and soon the crowning of our Holy Lord Bezos as dictator of Earth (if he hasn't managed to colonize Andromeda by that point).

The best way to niche down is to employ what is called layering. This refers to catering to as many specific interests as possible. A good example is this: Dog training is a broad niche. It implies you will train dogs, that's it. Compare this to labradoodle puppy training aimed towards female owners between the ages of 30-55 who are highly paid executives and earn at least $100,000.

Now, that is way more specific, isn't it? Your market size will shrink, but this is a good thing! If the demand exists, it means you're reducing your competition by niching down. Thus, your path to domination is easier. When speaking of online businesses, remember that you have the whole world at your disposal. Even a 'small' subniche will probably have at least a million people in it.

So always niche down and get as specific as possible. Layer as many interests and qualities as possible and evaluate their demand.

———

Build your Sales Funnel

Now that you know what you're going to sell and have niched down, all that remains to be done is to build your sales channel. Well, not quite, but it's the next step anyway. Your sales channel is how you will entice customers and sell them your product. A lot of first-time entrepreneurs think that if their product is good enough, people will come.

Well, this is simply not the case. It might be true if you are large enough, but even in that case, you need to let customers know that your product exists. Every prospective customer you receive will be at different levels in terms of making a buying decision.

———

There will be some who have done a lot of research and just want the product. On the other hand, we those who don't know the product and are just curious for information. The stages at which these customers exist is referred to as the buying stage cycle, and your engagement with them at every stage makes up your sales funnel. A sales funnel is best illustrated in figure 1.

Figure 1: A Sales Funnel

The uppermost level of the funnel is where your least engaged customer lie. These people are either just browsing or know very little and are not convinced they need to buy your product. The lowest level, which is also the smallest, are the most engaged customers who have read reviews, have done research, and need very little convincing to buy your product.

When selling, here's a tip that will save you countless man-hours: Focus on the tip and up to two levels above that. Forget about everybody else. Your website and sales copy should target customers who are already engaged with your product and are actively looking for a solution. Your job is to convince your potential customer that your answer is the best, not your competitor's.

Think about this: If you make cars, sell to those who are

looking for a vehicle. Don't market to folks who don't even know what a car is or prefer trucks. Convince them to trust you, not your entire line of business.

There are some simple steps you ought to follow in your sales copy. First, use a compelling headline that draws in eyeballs. This is your introduction to your customer and a crucial part of your copy. Avoid anything too flashy and succinctly express the problem you are addressing.

Next, engage your audience by talking more about the problem and propose your solution. Make an emotional connection with your customers. For example, when Skype needed to market its solution, they didn't just say "call people on the internet for free," their ads delivered the message that you could speak to your loved ones where ever they are at the click of a button. One of their earliest ads was a traveling father talking to his five-year-old daughter, who was making cupcakes. I mean, I know I'm being manipulated here, but it sure did bring a smile to my face!

Once you've done this, pitch them your offer backed by a strong guarantee. At this point, your customer is going to have all sorts of objections popping into their head, so add testimonials to convince them of how great your product is. Finally, ask for the sale. Always. Ask. For. The. Sale. Create urgency by giving them an offer that expires soon, or if your product has limited quantity, then mention this.

If all of the above is too much information, do this: Define your customers' buying cycle levels and figure out how deep your sales funnel goes. Refine it and then outsource the work to a professional copywriter.

Keep your design simple and collect your prospective customers' emails by using an opt-in form. An opt-in form is where a customer willingly "opts-in" by giving their email in exchange for an offer from you, like a news-letter or other updates. I'll explain why this is important shortly.

———

Drive Traffic

This principle dovetails with the previous point, but I'd like to reiterate how important it is for you to make sure you're being heard and letting people know your product exists. Don't think "if I build it, they will come," and such nonsense. Advertise and always work on driving engaged audiences to you.

. . .

You should focus on both free and paid traffic. Initially, paid traffic will be your primary source of audiences, so don't hesitate to spend money on this. Once your popularity grows, you'll see your organic traffic pickup. Google and other social media channels are excellent sources of this.

————

Provide Value

It is a given that your product or service needs to be good in order to make your customers happy and have them coming back. This sort of obvious thing is not what I'm talking about in this book. Value goes far deeper than merely having a good product.

Value refers to what you give your customers at each and every stage of your sales funnel. The benefit you provide them, via information or giveaways, should only have one goal: to keep them moving forward and increasing their engagement with your business.

Free content is the first and most obvious step in this process. You will need to produce copy which drives your least engaged customers to give you their email. Usually, in return for their email, businesses provide an eBook or research report or any such information which helps them. What most companies then proceed to do is to spam the inbox of this person, trying to brute force their way into the customer's consciousness.

Needless to say, this is the wrong way to go about things. You should always provide value since this is the easiest way to increase engagement. Once you've offered free content, a live demonstration via webinar or Facebook live, and so on, is a great tool to get them further engaged.

You could also consider providing free samples to your customers of either your product or a reduced version of it. Software companies do this all the time via free trials or limited features on free software. You want to be careful here and not limit the elements too much since this might turn off a customer.

Always provide value, and you'll notice your customer base increasing constantly. What's more, you'll also be able to build loyalty amongst your existing user base.

Be Visible

A key aspect of marketing that has emerged since the dawn of social media is the art of staying visible. The higher your visibility, the more you are in the consciousness of your customer. Earlier visions of this were by using paid ads that targeted customer interest, and these ads would popup wherever the customer went.

This idea was so overused that customers now are blind to such ads. So, what's the solution? Well, luckily we have Gary Vee to thank for a readymade solution:

> "If you're not creating content and distributing it on social media ... you're fundamentally irrelevant."- Gary Vaynerchuk

The key here is the words "creating content" and "social media." Content is ultimately what conveys value to your customers. Best of all, it's free since posting something on a social media outlet doesn't cost a thing. The key to engaging content is emotion, as in, stuff that generates positive feelings within them.

You need to utilize all of your social media channels to create engaging content to remain in your customers' consciousness. Even if you have a physical business, you need to be social. Use influencers, use funny photos,

whatever it takes. Keep driving those engagement numbers and generate positive emotions.

This sort of thing is way easier for some businesses than others. For example, a pet store is more likely to have higher engagement numbers than an accountant. It is important that you figure out what a good engagement number is and what your desired positive emotion is. For an accountant, the one emotion you need to generate is that of safety. Focus on that and keep hammering it home via your preferred outlet.

You don't need to be present on every channel, just the appropriate ones. It's better to have depth as opposed to width if you get what I mean.

———

Drive Repeat Purchases

The key to repeat customers for your online outlet is simple: Email marketing. All those emails you've been collecting are a veritable pot of gold for your business. Think of all the things that we connect to our emails. In an age when obsolescence is overtaking almost every-thing, the first invention of the internet age, an ordinary email, remains one of the most powerful communication tools.

Newsletters, thank you notes, birthday wishes, event-driven wishes are all great ways to increase engagement and move people along your sales funnel. Again, remember always to provide value and don't ask for more information than you need. It pays to be ethical in the long run, and your customers will appreciate it.

For example, if you need just the person's first name, don't ask for a last name or phone number. Honesty works because it is the biggest provider of value out there and the biggest generator of positive emotions when it comes to a business. Trust, happiness, and security are just some of the feelings that are generated, so always provide that.

Meanwhile, keep practicing proper marketing techniques with your email list. I would go so far as even buying email lists or solo ads as they're called from reputable vendors to increase your customer base. Never underestimate the power of the simple email and use it to your advantage!

―――――

Learn the Art of the Upsell

The upsell and the backend sell are one of the worst understood things out there. I'd go so far as saying the quality of the upsell determines how legitimate a business is about providing value and is a good indicator of how competent it is.

The online world is now plagued by a number of products, such as courses, and they all have a ton of upsells. The advertisement says 'only' $49, but once you purchase it, you find out that you need to pay $1000 more to access the real stuff. Even worse is when you pay and then discover that all of the 'unlocked' material is just really obvious.

This is particularly problematic since it technically isn't fraud, even if it is ethically. An excellent example of this is a popular affiliate marketing training website that provides initial information for free and then asks for a recurring yearly payment for generic and outdated training.

The easiest way to figure out upsells is by applying one 'do' and one 'don't': Do provide value with your upsell and don't be a scumbag. It really is that simple. Even backend sales, which are like the candy and gum which surround grocery store checkout aisles should provide value to your customer and accessorize their primary purchase.

Focusing on these two things will generate good cash flow for you, and the margins on these products and services tend to be higher than your main product. So always focus on developing these channels to boost your sales and profits.

This brings to a close our look at the pattern of profit. Follow this pattern and execute every point well, and you'll tilt the odds in your favor massively. Once that happens, remember that it doesn't matter if each individual action ends in success or not, the larger picture will always make you money. Speaking of money, that brings up a whole host of other issues, so let's look at that now.

TRACKING

So, let's talk about money, or to be more specific, tracking the metrics associated with the money in your business and how to make sense of it all. If you want to be successful in business, you need to be able to read financial statements and prepare rudimentary ones.

While you don't need to earn a CFA license, you should be able to look at the essential metrics and get a feel for how things are going. This sounds more difficult than it actually is because, trust me, once you start running your business, you'll understand things instinctively.

. . .

This chapter is meant to function as your guide to understanding the simple concepts that govern profitability.

FINANCIAL STATEMENTS

Briefly, there are three statements that measure the health of a business. They are the balance sheet, the income statement, and the cash flow statement. The cash flow statement is a more recent invention, comparatively, since the income statement is open to all sorts of accounting shenanigans.

The balance sheet simply lists the assets and liabilities of your business, along with the equity present. Let's not worry about equity but focus instead on what an asset is and what a liability is. An asset produces income for your business, and a liability is one that costs you money. Please note, I'm not sticking to the accounting definitions here. I'm giving you the real-world scenarios.

Unlike with accounting definitions, I tend to think of assets and liabilities as interchangeable, depending on how much of a return they are generating. For example, let's say you run a retail store where you sell eyeglasses and run an online outlet as well. The rent for the physical premises is a significant expense compared to the cost of the website. If you've borrowed money to pay for the premises, technically, those premises are a liability.

Let's make this even more interesting by supposing that the majority of your sales come online. So, with this information on hand, why on earth would you hang onto the liability that is the physical store? Well, let's examine how people purchase prescription glasses and sunglasses. Almost everyone tries them on. In some places, you can get a quick eye exam done. Perhaps, a lot of people wish to physically try out these glasses, and only then are they comfortable enough to place an order? Thus, your liability (which is how it will be recorded on your balance sheet) is actually an asset.

Inventory, which is the financial value of the products you currently have, is an asset from an accounting perspective. However, if your inventory is obsolete, it is a liability. My point is, always think of assets and liabilities in terms of how much return you're getting for your money from them. Be aware that an asset can turn into a liability and vice versa.

The income statement measures how profitable you are by listing your revenue, which is total sales, and then subtracting your running expenses to give you a bottom-line figure, which is your profit or income. This statement is very misleading; there isn't a single serious business person who relies on this to gauge the health of their business.

The reason is simple: the costs can be manipulated. For example, the rent you pay can be removed from operating costs since; technically, it is payment towards an asset. How you value your inventory affects the cost price of your goods and raw materials. Then there are non-cash items such as depreciation, which I'm not even going to bother getting into. My point is, the income statement is something you need to worry about and prepare only if you have investors. If your investors happen to be dumb enough actually to believe everything on there, seek funding elsewhere.

This brings me to the cash flow statement. The cash flow statement is the exact opposite of the income statement. This measures the cash inflows and outflows in your business. It lists out the cash expended to create assets, cash used to pay off debt and income generated from any interest-bearing deposits, and so on. Thus, it makes it easy to compare how much cash your business is generating after all expenses, and it gives you the choice of what to include or exclude depending on your judgment.

For example, we are going back to our spectacles shop. You can either consider the rental payments as operating expenses (opex) or capital expenditures (capex), which is what expenses towards building assets is termed as.

Capex is usually not subtracted from income, but depending on the business, capex can be an actual expense.

For a company such as Intel, for example, which needs to conduct regular research and keep improving its products continually, research expense, which is capex, should be subtracted from the cash flow from operations and sales. This is because, without that capex, there is no income.

Now, the topic you're interested in is not business valuation; it is your own business you're worried about. So, having established a base, let's now look at how you measure the health of your online business.

Metrics for Success

The way to determine your business' true earnings is very straightforward. You need to subtract the cash flow out from the cash flow in to arrive at this figure. The cash flow out will be a combination of opex and capex. Should you include capex in this figure?

Well, I'd say at the start you should because you won't have a definitive idea at this point as to how much you will need to reinvest to keep the business going. A business such as affiliate marketing doesn't demand too much capex every month, and whatever you do spend will probably occur every six months or so.

However, the opex of an affiliate marketing business will be high and mostly in the form of advertising or salaries for your virtual assistants (VAs) or any software you might be using. If you produce your own software and sell it via other affiliate marketers, you'll need to keep reinvesting, and your capex will be high. So, in these cases, you will need to include this number.

The key metric to focus on is your net profit. Net profit is the amount that you make after deducting all costs, including taxes, from your overall revenue. This can be expressed in two ways: as a percentage and as a number. As a percentage, net profit is simply the percentage of revenue that you're making as profit. Once your online businesses get rolling, this will be a high percentage, regularly above 20%.

However, the percentage doesn't matter much as a metric since you need to be concerned with the amount of net profit you're making a month. It is this second metric you need to keep a rigorous eye on since this is the one that determines whether or not your business is going to succeed. It is where your reinvestment money is going to come from, so your focus when starting any online business should be to ramp this up as soon as possible.

Here's an example: let's say you're starting a KDP business and invest $1000 to launch one book, in the audiobook, eBook and paperback formats. Now, let's say your keyword research is excellent, and you're making $250 per month from this book. Great! Within four months, you'll break even with this book, and after that, it's all profits.

Let's take stock after a year. You've made $3000 worth of revenue on a book that has cost you $1000 to produce. You did some advertising throughout and this cost you $500 for the whole year. So, your net profit is: Net profit amount = 3000-1000-500= $1500. Net profit margin = 1500/3000 = 50%.

While that net profit margin looks great, it hides the fact that you've made just $1500 over the course of an entire year. What's more, since you haven't reinvested for a whole year, your sales will almost certainly start flagging now, and there's no way you can maintain those profit numbers.

This is why, with every online business, it pays to start with a decent amount of capital. You need to scale up quickly and boost your net profit amount and not worry so much about your net profit percentage.

It is crucial for you to track your net profit amounts, and you can do this either by maintaining excel spreadsheets yourself or by using online software that will do the accounting for you like Zoho books or QuickBooks. Don't fall into the trap of buying into the net income hype and focus solely on the net profit amount.

This may seem to be a painful thing to do, but remember, you cannot improve what you don't track. Keep tabs on this number and seek to maximize it at every stage until it reaches a level you're comfortable with. Once it reaches that stage, take stock of the amount of reinvestment needed to maintain it and then figure out how to stabilize your margins.

Maximize

Creating more profits is simple. You simply follow the steps that maximize it and then repeat it over and over. Increasing profit is at the heart of every business, and again, this is a chaotic variable. You never know at the beginning, which of your efforts are going to have the biggest payoff.

That's the reason that you need to come up with as many solutions as possible and then track everything. Once this is done, focus on those efforts which are giving you the best bang for your buck and repeat that model over and over.

Just like with evaluating and starting a business successfully, there is a pattern of actions you can take that will tilt the odds in your favor.

TIPS TO PROFIT

Without any further ado, here are the best practices for you to increase profit. Remember that this applies, like a pattern, to all businesses, and it is by constantly repeating these actions that you can generate higher amounts of profits.

———

Eliminate

This tip particularly applies to service-based businesses, but product-based ones can take a lot from this too. When first designing your processes, you will end up adding a lot of things that are not useful to the customer. Of course, this happens not on purpose but out of good intentions.

However, a lot of entrepreneurs fail to go back and review their business processes and end up leaving a lot of these useless things in place, thereby reducing the overall value provided to the customer. For example, if you run a dropshipping business, does your customer really need to provide their exact order number when inquiring about the status of a shipment?

Would it not be easier for them to simply give you their registered email address and for your staff to track which shipment they're talking about? One of the people's pet peeves is to go back in and dig up the exact order number from their email, and sometimes people end up deleting them by mistake. Despite this, it is entirely possible on the backend to track the relevant shipments. So why ask for it in the first place? Yes, it adds an additional step for you, but really, does it add an extra 24 hours or something ridiculous like that? Hardly.

Eliminate processes and other accessories that do not add value. This is akin to fat, which adds nothing, and it is your duty to strip it off. The same applies to internal company processes. Think of your employees as customers and make it as easy as possible for them to come to work and do their jobs.

———

Smell What Sells

Cutting the fat involves removing products and services your customers don't want. The mistake that happens when designing services the customer doesn't want also occurs with products. There are many products that you will think are amazing and true game-changers but your customers, the ones giving you their money, don't think so.

Many companies have pushed ahead with terrible products despite market feedback that the consumer did not want or particularly care for these products. Examples such as the Ford Edsel and New Coke come to mind. Never ignore what the market is telling you and always remember, unless it violates your ethics, always gives the customers what they want and give them more of it.

It is easy to fall into the trap of trying to lecture your customers, and you need to resist it in order to succeed.

Value Your Time

Valuing your time goes beyond simple time management. It cuts to the heart of deciding what is a good use of your time and what isn't. Now, as you progress along your business journey, the tasks that were formerly a good use of time might turn into inefficient applications of your time. This is perfectly normal.

You see, every action you take for your business has a particular monetary value attached to it. For example, when I first began my KDP business, I used to format and design the book covers myself. This used to save me around sixty dollars overall, and in the case of books with a lot of images, it used to save me around a hundred. At the time, since I was fully dedicated to my KDP business, it made sense to cut costs as much as possible and exchange my time in return.

However, once the money started really rolling in and I diversified to other businesses, it didn't make sense anymore for me to spend a few hours doing these tasks instead of focusing on making more money via my other income streams. This is at the crux of a successful business: Spend your time doing what will make you the most money.

Sometimes, this time will need to be spent on cutting costs and trimming fat; sometimes, it will be on increasing your top-line revenue. Let your instincts guide you and always look at this from the risk to reward perspective.

———

Understand Cash Flow Patterns

Every business has a certain rhythm of cash coming in and going out. Look at your data long enough to understand this pattern and then plan and project into the future. Always keep making plans for future investment, either into your business or into another venture.

Here's the thing: Your first projections are going to be rubbish. You will underestimate costs, overestimate revenue, and the things you think will happen will not even come near the realm of possibility. Like with any other skill, you need to learn how to get better at this, and the only way to improve is to keep practicing.

Always keep cash flow at the top of your mind since this is the lifeblood of your business. Remember that sometimes, it is worthwhile to go into a bit of a hole in the present in order to realize a higher cash flow during peak sales periods. For example, the holiday season at the end of the year is a major shopping period.

If you're sitting in August or July, it might be worth it to reduce your cash reserves down to its minimum amount to prepare products for that peak season. Your overall profits will increase and will more than make up for the temporary hold you found yourself in. That is a scenario with a good risk to reward ratio.

Master Price Increases

Is one of your products selling well? Yes? Well, go on and increase the price then! Don't make the mistake of jacking up the price too much but a little bit, so that you don't adversely affect the demand.

Price increases need to be carried out very carefully since the customer is well aware of what is going on and will resent being taken advantage of. However, this goes back to you believing in yourself and the product you've created, so don't be afraid to increase the price and track what happens next.

Often, you'll see price increases affect sales in a manner you won't expect. You might see sales drop at the higher price significantly, and when you revert the amount back to its original level, you'll see higher sales than previously. You don't know where the money is going to come from, so always follow the pattern of maximizing profit with your products.

———

Educate Your Customer

Your customers often don't know what they want. This is typically the case for more mature businesses that have a few core products and are seeking to develop ancillary services to complement those products. The value of those services will be evident to you, but don't expect your customers to understand them right off the bat.

This situation is much like when a tune gets stuck in your head, and you begin to tap the table in what you think is that tune. Why don't you go ahead and do this? Think of a theme in your head and tap it on a desk and ask someone near you to guess which song you're beating out.

Chances are they'll think you're simply tapping out a random series of bangs on the desk. If they don't know the tune, they cannot guess it. Your customers are the same way. They don't have the information that you have, and instead of thinking of them as stupid or dim, educate them and give them value by creating new products and services which complement the existing ones you have.

———

Get a Grip on Costs

While the maxim of cutting costs to the bone is a good one, you must remember not to cut costs at the expense of quality. Remember, if you pay peanuts, all you'll get are monkeys. It is worthwhile to spend a little bit more on some occasions.

The crux of the issue is how well you can evaluate risk versus reward. A particular problem with online businesses is the decision to hire someone full time versus outsourcing work to a freelancer or a virtual assistant (VA). While the latter choices will be cheaper, you need to make sure you're getting good quality work in return.

Inventory poses a similar challenge. In dropshipping models, you can either order the products in advance and have it stored for immediate shipment in a warehouse, or you can have it manufactured and shipped on demand. The former increases your cost but also increases customer satisfaction. The latter reduces cost, but there is a long lead time to contend with.

Remember to derive as much value as possible from the costs you incur. Everything in your business is about the return you receive for your investments. Your costs are simply the investment you're making, and your profit is the return. Seen from this angle, your costs will make a lot more sense, instead of blindly cutting them to the bone.

———

Let Your Money Make You Money

Warren Buffet has often described his and his partner, Charlie Munger's, jobs as being one of deciding the ideal capital allocation for their companies. Indeed, this and evaluating risk is the primary function of every CEO out there. As the founder of your business, your job is no different.

By smart capital allocation, you can make the best returns on your investment and generate the highest amounts of profit for your business. A lot of entrepreneurs tend to fall into two distinct groups. Those who prefer to have cash in the bank and those who cannot stand to see it sitting there.

Well, neither approach is ideal. You have to find the perfect balance between spotting an opportunity and having enough cash on hand to take advantage of the opportunity. If you spot a good niche for your business to expand into, you can't do anything about it unless you have enough cash to operate within it. So always value your cash and realize what its true purpose is.

———

Evaluate Your Team

How good is your team? What is the quality of the people that work for you? Are they dependable, or are they cheap labor, which works erratically? Your business is only as good as the people involved, and even if you don't have a full-time roster of employees, the freelancers, and VAs who work for you determine the output of your business.

Always surround yourself with good people and make a commitment to get the best value for your investment in them.

You know what? I think I will devote an entire chapter to this topic instead of a single section.

THE TEAM

Your employees will determine the quality of the experience your customers have. Even if you sell through a channel, the people you hire to work for you will be the determining factor for the quality of the products you put out there. As much as your focus ought to be on the outside, with your customers and product, you need to devote time within as well.

Evaluating the quality of the people you have hired and setting systems in place to hire the right people in the future is the focus of this chapter.

YOUR PEOPLE AND YOU

If you already own a business, your first step is to check with yourself whether you would enthusiastically rehire all of your current employees. If the answer is for sure a yes, then good job. If there are some people you are not enthusiastic about, instead of casting them aside, genuinely give them the chance to improve.

Remember that as the leader of your company, you are mainly responsible for setting the tone. Ask yourself whether you've been slacking off in this regard or perhaps whether you haven't communicated well enough with your employees. You need to secure a buy-in from your employees, and they need to receive value from the work they do as well.

When I use the word employees, I'm referring to free-lancers and VAs (Virtual Assistants), as well. Everyone you pay money to for work needs to receive value. An old school of thought is that money itself provides more than enough value, but that isn't the case and frankly, never has been.

Your employees need to feel secure and need to know that you're capable of handling any problems that come in the way of the business. As such, you will sometimes see employees testing you by trying to push your buttons. This should not be taken personally, and you should instead view this as an opportunity. Such employees, in my experience, often turn out to be the most loyal and productive.

The ones you do need to worry about are those who insidiously undermine the company culture. If such a person happens to be an excellent worker, you should still, rid yourself of them because of the damage and negativity that such an employee brings outweigh any positives from their performance.

I'm not saying you should aim at starting a cult and insist on your employees buying into it. That would be an extremely nutty example. Neither should you choose to foist your own principles of work onto your employees without their buy-in. Writing books on the principles of work may work for Ray Dalio, but until you reach his level, stick to simply providing your employees with value and a pleasant workplace.

Some entrepreneurs go overboard and fill the workplace with all sorts of nonsense, which only provides distraction and not value. Remember to stick to the middle path at all times between being overly lax with your employees and being a draconian overlord.

Once you've evaluated your current work processes, the next step is to implement a solid hiring plan. This is actually a very straightforward task to do. Your goal is to hire the top people for the budget you have. Follow the five steps detailed in the next few sections to ensure this happens.

———

Step One: Build the Job Framework

One of the key things you must learn to do if you don't already is to let your employees exercise their own creativity in the workplace. To do this, you need to give them the big picture or outline and let them fill it with their own color. Chances are, they'll do something you haven't thought of and increase the quality of work.

To build a framework, you need to define the elements that are a part of the job function. Your first step is to start by identifying what the job function is. Don't get too granular with this and define the essence of the job function. An example is to say, "improve the quality of customer relationships" instead of saying "build relationships with supplier X by doing this and that…"

By defining the essence of the job, you are providing the

outline not just to yourself but to the employee you will eventually hire. Let them figure out the specific tasks that need to be done and let them define what a good relationship is exactly.

Your next step is to define the outcomes of that role. A lot of bosses go about this the wrong way by thinking of things related to their business in terms of goals. It's not the goals you want to achieve but outcomes. Outcomes are why you spend all those hours at work and refining things.

Get your employees thinking in the same manner, and their work will align itself accordingly. You need to be specific with your outcomes, so define them accurately. Use numbers or targets to define this as accurately as possible. There never should be any doubt as to whether you've hit a mark or not. So, statements such as "increase revenue" should be replaced by "increase revenue by 10% as compared to the previous year". Another good example is to replace "increase customer satisfaction by 10%" with "increase positive feedback from customers by 10% and decrease waiting times by 10%," and so on.

The latter example applies especially to customer service roles, and it is imperative that you have the correct people present there since they are the faces and voices of your company. It is crucial to set outcomes that are challenging but achievable. This can be a tough thing to get right, and

I'm afraid trial and error is the best method of finding that right balance.

The last step is to define the qualities expected of the employee. How will they conduct themselves and represent the company? What traits will they have? How do you see them helping and improving the culture at work? Define everything. This way, you give the employee a chance to exercise their creativity and also give yourself the best opportunity to evaluate prospective candidates in a fair manner.

————

Step Two: Source Intelligently

A lot of entrepreneurs post their job openings on job boards and then sit back and evaluate resumes. While this approach has its benefits, it isn't the most efficient method of doing things. The first step to take when looking to hire new people is to be proactive.

Go out, looking for candidates instead of letting them come to you. Start within your own network and inquire whether they know anyone who fits the bill. Some of the best hires are made via networking. Incentivize your own employees to refer people they know to the position.

This has the consequence of killing two birds with one stone since it gives employees greater familiarity with their workplace and creates a more harmonious environment. Give bonuses to existing employees for every successful new hire and thus create a peaceful and collaborative culture at work. Asking them to tap their networks for prospective hires is an especially good move since multiple sources will work better than just one.

Once this is done, try recruiters and headhunters. Now, I'm not a huge fan of doing this since the incentive structure within headhunting is all wrong. The headhunter's primary incentive lies in referring candidates who have high salaried positions to increase their own commission. I'm not judgmental here; it's just the way it is.

You might find them less enthusiastic about finding the right candidate for a lower-level position who also needs to fit the bill with regards to assimilating to the type of culture you have currently. This is why it is crucial you tap your network and those of your employees. If the position is critical enough, use the services of a recruiter. Otherwise, I wouldn't bother.

One way of solving the hiring issue is to develop internal capabilities and an internal recruiting department. This will certainly bring all the incentives in line. Hiring someone with a background in recruitment and incentivizing them in line with your goals, as per the framework in step one, is an excellent way to go about this.

Of course, we're talking about setting up an entire department here, and your company needs to be of a certain size for this to make sense. If your company is not at that size as yet, then it is best to use networking to source new candidates.

Once you've identified potential candidates, it is time to interview them. This brings up a whole another set of issues, so let's look at this next.

––––––

Step Three: Master the Art of Interviewing

Here's the deal: the way most companies approach the interview process is all wrong. The primary focus is always 'getting to know' the prospective employee. While this is an admirable goal, it fails to work for two reasons. One, you get to know the person, and if they have an agreeable personality, you can get swept away by it and end up ignoring the realities of what is needed for the position.

Secondly, this approach overvalues the need for someone to fit into the overall team culture. You want someone to be efficient and operate in a particular manner, not join a cult. A lot of entrepreneurs focus way too much on the importance of culture and not enough on their bottom line. As a result, in them screening out great candidates and hiring less than ideal people for the job.

Your ultimate goal should be to assess whether there are any red flags that could hamper your culture. The absence of a red flag is more than enough for a 'go' decision. Don't go looking for green flags with regards to cultural fit since this is a waste of time. Besides, the more diverse your workplace is, the better your quality of work will be.

The focus of your energies should be on evaluating competency. That is the reason why interviews are conducted in the first place. The best way to assess the absence of red flags and competence is to vary the kinds of meetings you lead. Traditionally, anywhere up to five interviews is thought to be the optimal number.

Each type of interview will give you a better idea of the sort of person the interviewee is. Always begin with a phone interview where you set the base. A good idea is to ask four or five major questions that are pertinent to the qualities necessary for the job and to structure them on the basis of "what and how". In other words, get them to provide you with as many tangible examples as possible.

Next, conduct an in-person interview, which will give both you and the candidate a better idea of what both of you are getting into. An important point to highlight here is that you cover the same ground as in the phone interview, via the same questions, but go into greater depth. The idea here is to look for inconsistencies and to get to the bottom of things you didn't get a clear picture on.

A lot of interviewers skip the questions in the phone interview and start all over again, and this is an indication of poor planning. Some companies try brain teasers and that sort of thing to measure creativity and performance under stress. While some of it might work, ultimately, there's no better indicator of performance under pressure than in-depth scrutiny of their personal work history. Make that your primary focus and leave the cute questions for later.

Your final interviews should be with the references the candidate has provided. Obviously, all the recommendations will be positive, so don't expect to glean a considerable amount of information here. Treat this as an opportunity to discern whether any red flags are present.

You can choose to conduct two more interviews, one where the team the candidate will be working with gets to ask questions and another where you recap all other discussions, and both of you take stock as to whether they're a good fit. A good idea is to schedule a full day visit and conduct all interviews on that day. This way, you don't stretch out the interview process too much, which might leave the candidate wondering how serious you are about filling the position.

Once the interviews are done, it's time to make a decision.

———

Step Four: Make a Decision

Once your interviews are done, correlate each candidate's

fit to the framework you previously prepared and check to see whether their competencies are a good match to your needs. This process helps remove any emotional decisions from the final decision.

Having said that, often, you'll find that your feelings for a particular candidate will alert you to certain conditions or red flags in ways that a scorecard or framework will not. So, don't ignore your emotions completely but be aware of why they are arising.

Be especially wary of people who have personalities you tend to get along well with. You should double-check to see whether such people have indeed produced any results or if these results were driven by piggybacking on other people's efforts. When checking references, pay special attention to what their coworkers say about them.

Often, you'll find that the person's manager is clueless as to what is going on within their team, and they'll be out of touch with the ground reality. Team members don't have this luxury since they need to execute the day to day tasks of the business, so always place greater weight on such evaluations.

Finally, place a grade next to each candidate and hire the ones with the highest grades. Understand that this whole process is not foolproof. However, it does reduce a lot of the mistakes that occur during the process and will save you from them.

Step Five: Market Yourself

This is not a step as much as it is something that must be done throughout the process. While the interview process is one where a candidate sells themselves to the company in question, the opposite equally applies. Unfortunately, a lot of companies ignore this and place themselves at a level above the prospective employee.

It is just arrogance and acting as if you don't need to extoll the benefits of working at your company is going to cost you in the long run. You'll end up scaring away the people who do have options and end up with those who desperately need a job, no matter whether they're qualified or not. Even worse, you'll be forced to pick from this pool exclusively since word will get around that you're not a great employer to work for.

Thus, always sell yourself to the candidate. Treat them with respect and outline the benefits they will receive by working for you. It is a good idea to apply this to those in your network you wish to bring on board, even if they seem to be happy at their current job.

Always keep tapping your network and use the resources available to you to keep probing and selling the great atmosphere at your workplace. Needless to say, make sure you actually provide those benefits and don't make something up out of thin air.

ONLINE BUSINESS SPECIFICS

Not everyone reading this works out of an office. This is one of the most significant advantages of an online business in that you can have staff working literally around the clock for you in different parts of the world. This can be done via freelancers and VAs.

One of the downsides to this is the fact that these people are not your employees, and as such, they don't have much invested in you. The best way to ensure good quality work is to have them provide you references. In the case of VAs, it is best to only work with those who come recommended to you and not going out and searching for new ones.

Sure, it is possible to find some real gems, but don't expand your VA circle until you already have a strong base of assistants you work with. The same applies to freelancers, but there are a number of tasks you can outsource, so this isn't a hard and fast rule. It is best to direct a good amount of work to a single person so as to assure them that you are a good source of income for them.

A constant source of worry for freelancers is finding their next gig. As long as you keep the work flowing in their direction, they'll be happy and provide you with better quality work. It is common for a freelancer to devote more significant time and resources to a bigger client than one who doesn't give them as much business, so take advantage of this.

A trap you can fall into is to think of the freelancer as your friend or employee. Remember that they are a business in and of themselves, so always make sure they're receiving some benefit, preferably monetary, for all of their actions. Don't expect them to work weekends just for you or go the extra mile because that's 'professional.'

Demanding such sort of things will quickly get you blacklisted amongst those networks, and you'll be forced to work with substandard people. So always value your relationships with them and keep things professional. If you have employees, it is vital that you outline your goals to them and provide a clear five-year or even ten-year path.

It doesn't matter if this is realized or not; the idea is to assure them that you know what it is you're doing. Your freelancers won't be as concerned about this, so make sure you pay them on time and keep sending steady work their way. A good idea is to refer other people to them and let them know about it so you'll develop more loyalty amongst them for you.

Your goals determine your path forward. I've touched upon this before, but now, it is time to take a more in-depth look at how to set proper and realistic goals and how to actually go about doing it. There are many different methods of doing this, but I can guarantee that the process I'll describe in the next chapter will ensure your success and get your employees inspired.

THE BIG PICTURE

Let's talk about goals. Those mythical things that everyone has and which everyone says you need to have in order to succeed. A goal is a target that gives you something to aim at or else you're going to find yourself and your company wandering aimlessly, not knowing which way you're going or even want to go.

The problem with goals is that there are just too many of the damn things. There are short term ones, urgent ones, non-urgent but critical ones, long term, medium term; it's enough to drive a person mad!

. . .

In this chapter, I'm going to give you a simple system to work all of these out, and you'll never find yourself asking, "what should we do next?" ever again. The key to all of your questions is the BHAG.

THINKING LONG TERM

The world of business, and indeed everything else, is changing at a lightning-fast pace these days. In such a world, where we don't know what is going to happen next month, thinking long term can seem detrimental to your strategy. However, it is thinking long term that helps you see the forest for the trees within the short-term fluctuations of circumstances.

By having a clear long-term target, you align and focus everything within your company towards that one goal and can drive towards it. Of course, it is not that easy. How do you choose a long-term goal? Should it be big? What if you don't reach it?

Well, the answer is simple: Don't set goals, set BHAGs! The concept of a BHAG (pronounced bee hag) stands for Big Hairy Audacious Goal and was first outlined by Jim Collins and Jerry Porras in their book *Built to Last*:

Successful Habits of Visionary Companies. The BHAG is a long term, think ten to twenty-five years, goal which cuts right to the heart of your company's purpose and values.

The key thing to understand is to grasp the big, hairy, and audacious part. The target you set must seem unrealistic, and you should feel as if it is unlikely you'll achieve it. It should be daring enough to generate positive energy within you and your organization, and it should be hairy enough for you to think that you could never sort out all the problems that this goal will throw your way.

Getting the degree of audacity is the key here. You see, it is simple to set unrealistic goals. Anyone can sit down and set a goal to be the richest person in the world within the next twenty years. However, deep down inside, there is a voice that will tell them that this goal is nonsense and that there's zero chance of them achieving it. This will bring a wave of negative emotion within them.

Your goals are not supposed to make you feel bad! They are supposed to inspire you and get you to consider the possibilities. You need to find that sweet spot where you think, "Whoa, that's impossible," and at the same time, think, "Wow, achieving that would be incredible!"

In short, look at it as two circles, one representing the impossibility and the other representing the positive emotion that is generated when you think of achieving the goal, intersecting. That is where you need to place your BHAG. For example, with the scenario where a person randomly sets a goal to become the richest person in the world, this is deep within the first circle and doesn't come anywhere close to the second.

An achievable goal, such as being able to go to the gym today or exercise in some manner, will not generate positive emotions within you since you don't consider it completely impossible. When you hit that sweet spot, the positive feeling that is created will propel you for a long time and energize everybody you work with.

––––––––

Qualities of a Good BHAG

If you asked me to tell you one thing that a BHAG absolutely must be, I'd say that it needs to be something that you may not realistically achieve. You might be confident of getting there about seventy or eighty percent of the way, but those last remaining steps seem impossible to cross.

It is vital that your goals have this quality because it adheres to something that has long been understood by all of us. If you plan for the stars, you still end up on the moon. You might not get where you aimed at, but you still go a long way forward from where you are. Setting an audacious goal will energize your organization and inspire everyone to give it their best shot.

By doing this, you solve a number of problems that occur at staid old companies such as employee motivation, burnout, turnover, and so on. These problems are just symptoms of a lack of inspiration amongst employees, and giving everyone a big goal to target will incentivize them to work harder and better. In short, your whole organization gets better.

The BHAG also has to be precise. In other words, the mission statement should be easily understood and not have any ambiguity. For example, become the greatest company in the world is extremely ambiguous. When do you plan on becoming the greatest company? What is great? And so on. Instead, be more specific and get into the details.

"In ten years, we will achieve revenue of X and profits of Y. We will be present in every home throughout XXX and will have captured X% or the market in YYY". Now, that is a very specific goal. Depending on where you're currently at, X and Y should be set at an audacious level, obviously. The key benefit of being particular is that it also makes your goal measurable.

Now, you don't need to provide the measurement metrics within the goal statement itself, but make sure to record it somewhere. For example, Tesla's mission statement is "to accelerate the world's transition to sustainable energy," which sounds like a vague statement, but you can bet they have clear metrics that define what "accelerate," "transition" and "sustainable" is.

By becoming measurable, there's no doubt as to whether or not you've achieved it. Thus, making it compelling and measurable gives a clear target for everyone to aim at and align themselves accordingly. Remember that the time-line should be long term, preferably at least ten years. You can extend this for however long you want, realistically speaking.

Remember that a good BHAG always lands in that sweet spot of sounding insane but sensible enough for you to believe that you can taste the fruits of achieving that goal.

———

Benefits of a Good BHAG

Beyond inspiring those within your business, a BHAG has other tangible benefits. For one, it gives your company a clear talking point at all times. Whenever someone meets you or asks you what your company does or asks the same of your employees, there is a clear mission statement to talk about.

Even better, the mission sounds a bit crazy, and that sparks further interest. It is a smart way of staying visible, which I talked about in the earlier chapter when discussing the pattern of a successful business. It provokes thought stirring conversations and will take you to interesting places.

You, therefore, give more meaning to your work because this goal is far more significant than what you currently are. Striving for something larger than yourself always inspires us to greater heights and is an excellent source of motivation. Your employees and even your customers are all a part of this grand vision, and you'll find it easier to secure buy-in from vital contacts and move people along your sales funnel.

Lastly, it inspires loyalty and trust within your team, and by keeping employee turnover almost nonexistent, you'll be able to create longer-lasting changes and development cycles. This ultimately results in better products and more satisfied customers, fueling your growth and bringing you closer to your target.

———

Types of BHAGs

There are different types of BHAGs, depending on the kind of goal you're shooting for. These are:

1. Target-oriented
2. Competitive
3. Role model inspired
4. Internal transformation

Target-oriented BHAGs can be either quantitative or qualitative in nature. A quantitative BHAG might be a revenue target. Generally speaking, quantitative BHAGs are a bit more challenging to inspire people with. You need to choose a large enough number to inspire people. One of the key qualities of a BHAG is whether your disappearance as the founder will still encourage the people working in the company to continue to strive for the goal or not. Qualitative BHAGs are easier to inspire people with, but make sure you define the metric with which you will measure them.

An example of a qualitative BHAG is "to become the dominant player in XYZ industry" or "to bring the world into the jet age," which was Boeing's BHAG back in the '50s. A quantitative BHAG is "to become a $XXX million company by YYYY."

The competitive BHAG is a great rallying cry but only works if you are the underdog. It gives everyone a common enemy to align against and can be a great war cry that accompanies everything that you do. There is a possibility of it hopping over into negative territory, so you need to strictly monitor the ethics of your actions if you're using this. A great example of this is Nike's BHAG in the 1960s, which was simply "Crush Adidas."

The role model BHAG is a more positive version of the competitive BHAG and conveys the same messages but across industries. With this BHAG, you can inspire your employees and organization to live up to an ideal and respected company. A good example is that of Giro sport design, whose BHAG way back in the 1980s was "become the Nike of the cycling industry."

The internal transformation BHAG is best suited for very large organizations that have multiple divisions and those that have a number of younger competitors coming after them. Whether it be to reinvent or re-energize the organization, this type of BHAG is an excellent motivation tool for larger companies or divisions. A good example is that of Merck back in the 1930s: "Transform this company from a chemical manufacturer into one of the preeminent drug-making companies in the world."

Choose an appropriate type of BHAG for your organization and make sure to review it annually to check up on progress. Of course, creating a BHAG is far more critical than merely studying it, so let's take a detailed look at how this works.

CREATING AND ACHIEVING
YOUR BHAG

There are steps you have to take to develop and achieve your BHAG. When done this way, you'll ensure that you go about it in an orderly manner and achieve the outcomes that the BHAG is supposed to inspire.

The first step is to think.

———

Deep Thinking

Determining your BHAG isn't something you can or should attempt to do overnight. It requires a lot of thought, and the way you word it is especially important.

Remember that there are multiple goals the BHAG aims to achieve, and you should not take this step lightly.

It might sound a bit strange to say this, but the one thing that a lot of people detest doing is to think. Thinking requires effort, and channeling your thoughts requires energy and is a habit that a lot of us aren't accustomed to. Thus, there will be a lot of resistance within you to carry out this step. However, it is necessary that you execute it nonetheless.

To better direct your thoughts, ask yourself the following questions:

In which activity or metric can your company be the best in the world?

What is your organization's core purpose? What is the biggest profit generator for your company?

This last question might seem out of place in what is a spiritual exercise, but it is a business reality. It is no good being great at something that no one is willing to pay for. You need to find the intersection points between these three questions in order to begin to develop your BHAG.

Meet regularly with your entire team to discuss and refine your objective. Involving your team is a great way to get them invested in the outcome of the process and also build commitment and loyalty to your organization. If given a stake in defining the goal for the company, they'll have more of an incentive to achieve it.

Again, don't assume that you'll come up with something overnight. In fact, don't put a timeline on it and let it find you. A good idea is to go out in nature or someplace where you can think and meditate upon this deeply. You'll find inspiration striking you soon enough.

––––––––

Validate It

Once you come up with a mission statement, put it to the test. Does it satisfy all the criteria required of a BHAG? Does it energize those you convey it to? Convey the message to your team and see how they react. Do they respond with enthusiasm or forced smiles?

Evaluate yourself and your feelings in reaction to reading the statement. Does it scare you a little? Does it energize you nonetheless? Can you see and imagine the benefits of achieving this goal and feel the rush of positive energy?

Remember that your BHAG needs to be measurable. Ask

yourself whether you've defined the metrics that will govern whether or not you've attained it. While a quantitative BHAG will have easy answers to this, this is not so effortlessly done in other cases. In competitive BHAGs, is your measure of success your own prosperity or your competitor's demise?

This seems like a small point, but you can appreciate how different both outcomes are. One is a positive goal, and the other will lead you into all sorts of unethical landscapes that are best to be avoided. How clear is your BHAG? Is it simple enough to be conveyed and understood by a primate?

You might laugh, but trust me, you will eventually run into someone in a position of influence who has the mental capacity of one, and it is crucial you be able to convey your mission to such dolts. It is a good test of how simple your message is and can also be a starting point for all of your advertising campaigns. However, that is not the primary purpose of this exercise.

———

Set a Due Date

When will you achieve this by? Once you set a due date, you start the clock, and now, you're fully committed to realizing your BHAG. You have no option but to start putting it into action, and this has the added effect of getting your creative juices flowing.

Much like how adding urgency pushes a customer closer towards the buy button, it will also drive you closer towards your goal. If you don't set a due date on it, your brain will classify this as an unimportant goal, and it is unlikely you will ever achieve it.

———

Communicate

This is the big moment where you officially unveil your BHAG to your entire organization and finalize it with your team. If you've done things right thus far, they should be energized by it, and you will be able to stream-line your hiring and staff evaluation by severing ties with those members who are not 100 % on board with this. You can not afford to have people on your staff that are giving not their all.

. . .

Again, it is vital for you to remember that your employees have their own lives and worries and that they are unlikely to be as motivated about the BHAG as you are. After all, they did not found your company. However, they do need to use it as a source of inspiration and be able to use it to drive themselves to a higher level of work.

An excellent way to measure this is to check the overall culture and work ethic of the organization once your BHAG is in motion. By work ethic, I don't mean whether your staff pull all-nighters or not. The amount of time spent at work is probably the most useless metric to track, and it is only the worst managers who do this.

Instead, keep a sharp eye on the quality of work being produced and check to see if it is on an upward trajectory. If it isn't, you likely have a few problems in your team's composition, and you need to either reevaluate your BHAG or recompose your team via new hires.

———

Develop Plans

Your BHAG is quite a long way away, so it is crucial to establish mile markers along the way to energize your team and to remind yourself of how far you've come and the remaining distance. Much like the purpose, vision, and goal framework we looked at in an earlier chapter, these mile markers serve to mark your progress.

The difference here is that your markers will themselves be medium-term in duration and will have to be broken down further into short term goals. You could have a mile-stone three years out, and those three years can be broken into smaller periods of a year each.

Resist the temptation to have more than two levels of goals. So, have a medium and a short term, and that's it. Don't further break down your short-term goals into shorter-term goals since this will only get everyone caught up in the specifics of these goals, and everyone will forget the BHAG.

The idea is to let the inspiration of the BHAG infuse everything that is done day-to-day, so make sure it is prominently in everyone's consciousness. This can be achieved via messages or quotes throughout the workplace.

Much like how your BAG is measurable, make sure your short-term goals are clear as well. You should be in no doubt as to whether or not you've achieved this target and as to whether you're ready to move onto the next one. Sometimes you'll have to revise your short-term goals, so don't worry about doing this.

Occasional revision is standard, but if you have to do this constantly, then it is a sign that your planning process is incorrect or that your BHAG has something wrong with it.

———

Inform Execution

As mentioned earlier, your BHAG should provide inspiration and impetus for all of your day-to-day activities. Use this to guide you with regards to all the decisions you make, be it hiring, firing, accepting new projects, or discarding old ones.

Trust your BHAG to guide you and commit to it, and you'll find yourself always clear-headed with regards to what to do next.

———

Reward Yourself

Don't remain in work mode all the time. It will feel amazing and have a positive impact when your organization reaches its BHAG. At the various mile markers, take some time to celebrate your success. Remind your team of how close they are to achieving the goals you've set for your organization together.

Celebrate challenges with positivity and embrace mistakes as negative feedback. This way, you'll always have an energized team that is motivated to achieve the BHAG.

And once you do get to your BHAG, remember to have some fun! Once that is done, start mapping out your next BHAG!

LEGACIES AND PROFITS

Throughout this book, I've been holding up profit as your primary goal and the one metric by which you can measure the success or failure of your business. Everything that we've discussed, from profit patterns to BHAGs to hiring your team, has been with the sole intention of maximizing your profit.

However, I'm going to pull the rug out from under your feet a little bit in this chapter by telling you that profits are not the only thing you should judge your business by. In fact, they are the second most important thing for your business.

. . .

The most important thing is: Impact.

PROFIT VS IMPACT

The dictionary definition of impact is "a marked effect or influence." You see, truly great products and companies don't just leave profits in their wake, they also leave a positive and life-changing impact. If you wish to put this in mercantile terms, impact is good business.

Now, I must stress that at the earlier stages of your organization, the impact you're creating should not be the primary focus. The best way to describe this is by saying that to change any system; you need to change it from within, not without. For you to be able to have the most substantial impact, you need to make money first.

Thus, if your primary product or golden egg is something that, for whatever reason, isn't creating much of an impact, this doesn't mean you pull it from the shelves or change your business lines altogether to develop something that is more impactful. No, this would be stupid in the extreme.

Instead, focus on other avenues of making an impact. For example, if you're a chocolate maker, why not try to source ingredients from more impoverished communities. This will benefit them and result in more product sales. A lot of retailers these days are pursuing the excellent initiative of donating a dollar for a specific sum of revenue that they generate, with some giving away products instead.

There are numerous initiatives like this where you can make a real difference. A strange thing happens to most entrepreneurs when they reach a particular stage of their business careers. Once enough profit is generated, every single one of them tends to turn their eyes towards humanitarian efforts and the betterment of communities.

This is one side of impact, of course. Creating a positive change in a world driven by your profits is a wonderful cause, and I believe it is something every person must do. However, this chapter isn't here to urge you to go and plant more trees or build more schools. No, charity is something that ought to happen by default at every stage of your life.

What I'm teaching you in this chapter is how to harness the power of impact to leave a lasting impression with your consumers and with that putting your profits on autopilot.

The Role of Emotion

Even if you don't want to admit this, and I'm looking at the men here, human beings are primarily driven by emotions. We don't fully understand where emotions come from, and thus, in what is an extremely human thing to do, we fear them and castigate them as a weakness. We only focus on their ability to cause us to make poor decisions and completely ignore how they often help us make the right ones too.

This is one of the reasons why I'm not in favor of adopting extremely rational work principles since it completely ignores emotional intelligence, which is necessary for any company to thrive. When selecting a work culture, it is crucial that your workforce be diverse, and I don't mean ethically or in terms of skin color either.

You need to embrace many different work styles and thought processes and direct them within a framework. Let them explore it and color it themselves, with your job simply being a high-level direction and making sure the structure is doing its job. The framework here is your BHAG.

Your BHAG has the added benefit of also helping your consumers adopt a viewpoint that benefits your goals. Now, you don't have to communicate your exact BHAG to the consumer. Indeed, this wouldn't always make sense to them, but the ethos of it should transfer over to your marketing campaigns and help you reel in consumers who are loyal.

The emotion that your BHAG generates within you and your employees is a valuable thing for you to harness and transfer over to your consumer. Take Apple, for example. Near the turn of the century, this was a company that had a tumultuous history with one of its founders being thrown out and then reinstated. It had not had a great product for a long time and was far behind Microsoft in terms of mental space with its consumers.

What Steve Jobs did, amongst many other things, was transfer the emotion he held for his products and vision, over to his employees, who then moved them over to the paying public. This was done via a BHAG, even if it wasn't titled as such. The release of the iMac, the iPod, and the iPhone are clear mile markers indicating steady progress towards the BHAG.

By the time the iPhone was released, Apple had not only displaced Microsoft, but it had also created an entirely new playing field with different rules, to the extent that companies like Google and Facebook were forced to change their working models. In case you don't remember, prior to the iPhone, Facebook was primarily a desktop application, and the word "app" hadn't been invented yet. They were still called programs.

This is an absurd turnaround for a company that in the mid-'90s, wasn't sure of what kind of a company it even was. The iMac was the first in a line of mile markers, which created a huge impact amongst its consumers, to the extent that some original iMacs are collectible items, especially ones with transparent casings and not colored like the majority were.

With every release, the impact generated upon the public increased, and the impact that Apple products create these days can be proved by the fact that fans still mob its stores despite the company not having released any revolutionary products since the earlier part of this decade.

It is worth dissecting the lessons of this a bit further.

———

Guaranteed Income

The first thing that is very evident from Apple's story is that their products are guaranteed to sell no matter how terrible they are. In fact, damaging leaks that Apple deliberately built obsolescence into their products to push their customers to buy newer releases barely made a scratch amongst the public.

Contrast this by pretending if such news was made public about Microsoft, and you'll see my point. Both companies occupy very different emotions when it comes to people's minds. You see, that impact creates the best kind of income, which is passive income.

Once your product changes people's lives or leaves a lasting positive emotion within them, they are guaranteed to come back for more. Mind you; they won't come rushing into the doors the minute you release the product. Impact takes time to build up, and consistency is the key.

The best way of ensuring consistency is quite simple. It is via your BHAG. This way, everyone in the organization is on the same page, and there's no second-guessing as to what the next step ought to be. Is it any wonder that almost every employee who was instrumental in designing Apple's products under Jobs sounds like they're parroting Jobs every time they speak?

This is the power of the BHAG when it is aligned for impact and not just profits.

———

Impact is the Best Advertisement

Which is a better advertisement for your product? A happy consumer or a slickly produced ad? In the short run, the latter will generate a lot more eyeballs, but the impact is about the long term. Much like the BHAG, the effect you seek to produce will manifest itself quite a few

years from now, and it isn't something you should expect
to see overnight.

Impact also helps you create better products in that it
helps you narrow down and focus on what the consumer
wants. How will it change their lives, and how much
easier will it make them? This is the best way to avoid
creating clones and marginally better products than what
is already available in the marketplace.

If you're taking on an established competitor, this is the
best way to proceed. Remember that for you to be able to
unseat a dominant competitor, it isn't enough to create
something that matches their product. It has to be something that blows the existing paradigm out of the water.

An excellent example of all these points is the story of
Lamborghini and how it came to be formed. Before
proceeding, I must warn you that extreme Italian
behavior is about to ensue. Anyway, in the 1960s,
Ferruccio Lamborghini was a successful tractor maker,
repurposing WWII military machines. This eventually
led him to purchase a Ferrari 250 GT. Thanks to its
numerous successes in racing, Ferrari's cars were considered the best in the world. This was despite the fact that
Enzo Ferrari publicly stated he didn't care about his
sports cars and only made them to generate money to go
racing. Talk about impact!

Anyway, it wasn't long after when Lamborghini had
problems with the clutch of his car, and this led him to

complain to the old man Enzo himself. Ferrari's reply was that the problem was not with the car but with the driver and that a tractor maker would not know anything about cars. Enzo might as well have insulted the man's family and called his grandma a horse.

Enraged, Lamborghini decided to commission the first build of his own car, which had a very simple, yet crazy goal: to reach 150mph on the autostrada that connects Milan to Naples. The Lamborghini 350 GT did this and was followed by the legendary Miura, which to this day, is considered one of the most beautiful and crazy cars ever made. Thus, Lamborghini's reputation for batshit insanity was born and was dutifully upheld by automobiles like the Eraco, the Countach, and the Diablo.

The impact Lamborghini's mad cars made exist to this day, despite the Italian marque being a subsidiary of the extremely German Volkswagen and turning out designs that are quite sensible compared to its history. While you fully expected older Lamborghinis to come equipped with machine guns, today's ones make do with simple bodywork slits and an exposed engine.

None of that matters though. The cars created an impact, and that impact fostered a reputation that sets it a cut apart from the rest. All the current owners of the marque do is push the envelope of craziness a little bit to keep the reputation going, and the brand thrives.

Impact Inspires the World

Getting back to our original example of Apple, there is no doubt of how much our lives have changed since the iPhone was released. That particular Apple conference is a true "where were you" moment. It almost seems wrong to sit down and coldly analyze why the iPhone was such a massive success because the positive emotion it generated was so high that we cannot help but look at it with rose-tinted glasses.

A lot of products throughout the course of history have generated such levels of emotion. Books are a great example. Look at any field of study, and chances are that you will find books printed in the early 1900s still being sold. Examples include works by Dale Carnegie and Napoleon Hill. A more recent example is Steven Covey, whose works have long outlived his demise.

By making the world a better place, you cannot help but generate positive emotions. This should not turn into an in-depth commercial analysis since you should strive for this goal automatically, but try to associate your product's goals with this aim. Your consumers will thank you for it, and you'll automatically ensure a legacy.

Lastly, having a positive impact aligned with your BHAG inspires your employees, as well. We're firmly in the millennial generation, and for all the stick that this lot takes from the boomers, there is no denying that this generation does not take the world for granted as their parents did.

Your employees are likely to be far more concerned with the positive impact your business has on the world, and you're more likely to attract and retain such people if you make the creation of a positive impact a part of your BHAG.

Use the power of emotion to help you reach your goals. The best part is, you'll end up making the world a far better place in return!

CONCLUSION

Well, it looks like you've made it to the end of the book! We started off by looking at why an online business is the best form of business and ended with an appeal for you to go out and change the world. It's been quite a journey!

Now get started by following the key points and patterns discussed in here. Always follow the profit pattern and remember the key thing about business: It is a chaotic environment, and you should always worry about tilting the odds in your favor instead of trying to guarantee profits and revenues.

Another concept I'd like to point out at this point is the Pareto principle, which states that everything takes place in an 80/20 ratio. Applied to business, what this means is that eighty percent of your results will come from twenty percent of your actions, and twenty percent of your results will come from the remaining eighty.

Once you've applied the profit pattern, always take the time to sit down and evaluate which are your key profit drivers. By doing this exercise, you'll be able to focus on the things that really drive your business and generate even more income.

Also, remember to surround yourself with a great team since you're only as good as the people you rely on for your business. There are many methods out there which promise you great results in terms of ensuring the best quality of people when hiring, but don't forget always to give value back to your employees.

Value, ultimately is what drives every business forward. The benefit you provide to your customers, what your employees receive by working for you and, last but not least, the value you derive by running a business. Impact is merely the concept of value taken to a higher degree, and thus, the higher the impact, the more everyone benefits.

If you're just starting out, focus on the earlier chapters in this book, which will give you what you need to not only start a business but to evaluate your performance and to fix the key points which will drive your profits. At this stage, you don't need to worry about impact as much as just remembering to provide value at every juncture.

If you run a medium-sized business already, the later chapters will be of huge value to you. Remember that at your levels, all improvements are going to be marginal, so even a seemingly small change will have a significant impact. It is vital for you to prioritize and classify what it is you wish to do via understanding the risk-reward return of every activity.

For those of you running larger businesses, it is time to think in terms of the impact you provide your consumers. This is the best way for you to ensure growth and to ensure a legacy, which is something that is not to be taken lightly.

No matter which level you're at, make sure you set appropriate BHAGs and take massive action to achieve them. Inspire those around you, and you'll find that the profits will follow.

I hope this book has been as wonderful an experience for you to read as it has been for me to write. Remember, I'm extremely keen to hear what you think of this, so do let me know how this book has helped you or changed your thinking in your review.

I wish you all the luck in the world. Now go out and achieve your dreams!

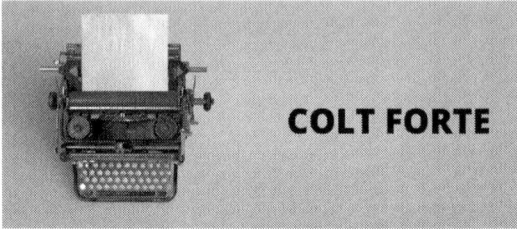

COLT FORTE

As an independent author with a small marketing budget, reviews are my livelihood on this platform.

If you are enjoying this book, I would appreciate it if you left me your honest review.

Thank you, Colt Forte

REFERENCES

Mindtools.com. (2019). *Emotional Intelligence in Leader- ship: Learning How to Be More Aware.* [online] Available at: https://www.mindtools.com/pages/article/newL- DR_45.htm [Accessed 12 Jul. 2019].

Fowler, D. (2017). *Women Are More Popular On Instagram Than Men According To New Study.* [online] Grazia. Available at: https://graziadaily.co.uk/life/real-life/instagram-study-gender-likes/ [Accessed 12 Jul. 2019].

Gazdecki, A. (2018). *Council Post: Why Progressive Web Apps Will Replace Native Mobile Apps.* [online] Forbes.com. Available at: https://www.forbes.com/sites/forbestechcouncil/2018/03/09/why-progressive-web-apps-will-replace-native-mobile-apps/#7faf848e2112 [Accessed 12 Jul. 2019].

Grant, A. (2015). *Originals*. 1st ed. Penguin Random House.

Long, M. and Lieberman, D. (2018). *Entrepreneurs' Brains Are Wired Differently. Here's How to Use Yours Right.*.[online]Entrepreneur.Availableat: https://www. entrepreneur.com/article/319761 [Accessed 12 Jul. 2019].

Maltz, M. (1960). *Psycho-cybernetics*. New York: Pocket Books.

gopher

Made in the USA
Monee, IL
11 May 2020